The Family Book

Creative Ideas for Christian Families

by Karen Holford

with contributions from Sam Davis, Cyril Sweeney and Richard Willis

Firstly, a big 'Thank you!'

Thank you to:

My husband Bernie Holford

My children Bethany, Nathan and Joel

My parents Kate and Tony Welch

My brother Tim, his wife Nita, and their children Matthew and Yasmin

My grandparents, Stan and Lily Welch, Edna and Bill Barber, and

Uncles Don and Tony

John Welch and family

John and Ruth Lennox

Annette and Phil Hubbard with Carissa

Phil and Lorena Lennox with Kelsey

David and Lisa Lennox with Sarah and Hannah

Alec and Hedy Holford

Alison and Michael Bo Jensen with Sebastian, Nathaniel and Helena

Graham and Janet

Colin and Marina

Robert and Jo with Jacques

Auntie Maud

And all the other people I know as family…

Thank you for the different perspectives on family you have each given me, which have blended together into creating this book.

Thank you for the amazing memories we have shared, and for the amazing love you have shown!

Lots of love, always,

Karen

Copyright © 2004

First published 2004, reprinted 2014

Design:

Abigail Murphy

ISBN 1-899505-93-8

Published by
The Stanborough Press Limited
Alma Park, Grantham, England

Printed in China

The Family Book

Creative Ideas for Christian Families

by Karen Holford

with contributions from Sam Davis, Cyril Sweeney and Richard Willis

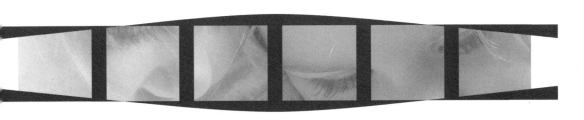

Contents

All Bible texts are from the New Internation Version unless otherwise stated
Versions • NRSV – New Revied Standard Version • NKJV – New King James Version

Introduction

Families are all different. They are various shapes and sizes and everyone in every family is different from everyone else. And yet God has put us all together, in multifarious combinations, to live as families and share in his love.

This book is not intended to be a 'How To . . .' manual for Christian family life. Rather, it is intended to help you reflect upon, and consider, your own family, with its unique needs and skills.

You will find lots of practical ideas among the pages, but they are there to inspire you and to stimulate you to develop your own ideas. You are the expert on your family, so you can browse among the pages of this book and take what is helpful for you, and leave the rest. Maybe the other ideas will suit your needs another time, maybe not.

It is my prayer that God will use this book to inspire you and your family as you live out his love in a very real way, every day of your lives together.

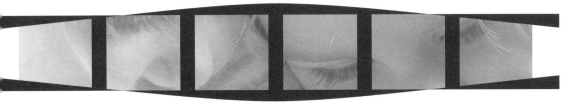

Chapter 1

Biblical foundations for nurturing relationships

Loving as God loves us

God is our Father and Creator and Jesus is our Brother. We are all brothers and sisters in God's family

- 'You are all sons of God through faith in Christ Jesus.' Galatians 3:26.

We are all equal – young and old, male and female, God sees us all the same

- 'There is neither Jew nor Greek, slave nor free, male nor female, for you are all one in Christ Jesus.' Galatians 3:28.

Jesus died to save us from our sins and to give us a hope in heaven

- 'For God so loved the world that he gave his one and only Son, that whoever

> Love is not about loving the deserving, but loving the undeserving as if they were the most deserving. This is the challenge of love in our everyday lives.

believes in him shall not perish but have eternal life.' John 3:16.

God lavishes us all with his love and grace, whether we deserve it or not

- 'How great is the love the Father has lavished on us, that we should be called the children of God! And that is what we are!' 1 John 3:1.
- 'For it is by grace you have been saved, through faith.' Ephesians 2:8.
- 'Because of his great love for us, God, who is rich in mercy, made us alive with Christ even when we were dead in transgressions.' Ephesians 2:4.

God fills us with his love so that we can love each other more effectively

- 'Be imitators of God, therefore, as dearly loved children and live a life of love, just as Christ loved us and gave himself up for us as a fragrant offering and sacrifice to God.' Ephesians 5:1, 2.
- 'Dear Friends, let us love one another, for love comes from God.' 1 John 4:7.
- 'We love because he first loved us.' 1 John 4:19.

Experiencing God's love for yourself

God loves us!
Read Psalm 103. Then list the ways in which God shows his love for you. Add other ways to your list, backing them with biblical references.

We love God
Write a love letter to God in response to his amazing love for you.

We are funnels of God's love to a hurting world
God is lavishing us all with his amazing love. We experience that love often through the way others show their love for us. Sometimes when we relate to others in an unloving way, it is as if we are holding a sunshade over their heads so that they can't experience God's love so effectively.

When we are loving and unselfish towards each other, then we are funnels, focusing God's precious love on those who are longing to feel his love, grace and acceptance.

Think about it
How can I be a funnel and not a sunshade as I help others to experience the love of God?

Relating to each other in a biblical way

Every relationship we have is a two-way experience. Whatever we do or say to others will affect the way they relate to us. We also respond to one another in different ways, with differing consequences.

Here are some biblical guidelines for encouraging healthy relationships:

Love each other
'Love each other as I have loved you.'
John 15:12.
'Be devoted to one another in brotherly love.'
Romans 12:10.

When you would like to show love
You might ask, 'What can I do today to show you how much I love you?' and then respond to the answer in the best way you can. Offer affection in a way that you know will be appreciated.

When you would like love to be shown to you
You might say, 'I feel really loved by you when you . . . . Please would you do that for me now?' or 'I feel in need of a hug right now. Please would you hold me?'

Have a thankful attitude to each other (Appreciation)

'I thank my God every time I remember you.' Philippians 1:3.

When you want to show appreciation

You might say, 'I really appreciate it when you do . . . .' 'It means so much to me when you take the time to do . . . .' Or you might send a note of thanks or appreciation. Be as specific as you can be about what you appreciate.

Comfort each other

'Praise be to . . . the God of all comfort, who comforts us in all our troubles, so that we can comfort those in any trouble with the comfort we ourselves have received from God.'
2 Corinthians 1:3, 4.
'Mourn with those who mourn.' Romans 12:15

When you would like to show comfort

You might say, 'I am so sad that you hurt so much. What would you find most comforting?'

When you would like comfort to be shown to you

You might say, 'I feel so sad, but I would really like it if you could . . . hold me for a little while . . . stay with me . . . help me by . . . etc.'

Respect each other

'Honour one another above yourselves.' Romans 12:10.
'In humility consider others better than yourselves.'
Philippians 2:3.
'Let us not become conceited, provoking and envying each other.'
Galatians 5:26.

'Each of you should look not only to your own interests, but also to the interests of others.' Philippians 2:4.

When you would like to show respect

You might say, 'What would you like to do?' 'What do you think about this?' 'Your opinion is important to me.' Avoid doing things that upset or offend the other person. Consider how your words and actions will affect those around you.

When you would like respect shown to you

You might say, 'Would it be possible for me to tell you what I think about this?'
'I have an idea that may help you.' 'Please could you consider my perspective?'

Encourage each other

'Encourage one another and build each other up, just as in fact you are doing.'
1 Thessalonians 5:11.
'Each of us should please his neighbour for his good, to build him up.' Romans 15:2.

When you would like to show encouragement

You might say, 'You are doing a great job! Don't give up! Is there anything I can do to help you towards your goal?'

When you would like encouragement shown to you

You might say, 'I'm feeling overwhelmed by this project at the moment, and I would really like it if you would be able to . . . .'

Accept one another

'Accept one another, then, just as Christ accepted you, in order to bring praise to God.' Romans 15:7.

When you would like to show acceptance

You might say, 'I want you to know that I love you, whatever you do. Even when you feel as if you have made a mistake, I'm still here for you, and I always will be.'

When you need acceptance

You might say, 'I know I'm not perfect, but I just need to know that you still love me.'

Support each other

'Carry each other's burdens, and in this way you will fulfil the law of Christ.' Galatians 6:2.

When you would like to show support

You might say, 'What can I do to help you?' You might offer to do one of their chores to give them extra time to do what they need to do.

When you would like support from others

You might say, 'Please can you help me?' or 'I have a problem I think you can help me with.'

Be at peace with each other

'Live in harmony with one another.' Romans 12:16.
'Live at peace with everyone.' Romans 12:18.

When you want to live peacefully, learn to listen to each other, respect each other's differences, and put the other's needs before your own. Take care to protect yourself from harmful conflicts.

Forgive each other

'Bear with each other and forgive whatever grievances you may have against one another. Forgive as the Lord forgave you.' Colossians 3:13.
'Confess your sins to each other and pray for each other so that you may be healed.' James 5:16.

When you would like to show forgiveness

You might say, 'I want to be able to forgive you

completely. It may not always be easy for me to do that, and I'm praying that God will help me to forgive you in the way he forgives me.'

When you would like forgiveness shown to you
You might say, 'I'm sorry that my words/my actions hurt you so much. I want to pray that God will help me not to hurt you like that again. I hope that you will feel able to forgive me when you are ready to do so.'

Be patient with each other
'Be patient with everyone.' 1 Thessalonians 5:14.

When you would like to show patience
You can show patience by giving others plenty of time to do what they have to do and say what they have to say. Try not to rush them or take over what they are doing. You might say, 'It's all right; take your time.'

When you would like patience shown to you
You might say, 'Please don't rush me. I just need a little extra time to understand/do this.'

Be kind to each other
'Always try to be kind to each other.'
1 Thessalonians 5:15.
'Be kind and compassionate to one another.'
Ephesians 4:32.
'Let us do good to all people, especially to those who belong to the family of believers.'
Galatians 6:10.

When you would like to show kindness
You might ask, 'What one thing could I do today to make your life easier,' and then do it. Find ways to surprise others with your love and thoughtfulness.

When you would like kindness shown to you
You might say, 'I would really appreciate it if you could find the time to do . . . for me.'

Thank you to Dr David Ferguson of Intimate Life Ministries for some of the ideas in this section. Intimate Life Ministries, PO Box 201808, Austin, Texas, 78720-1808, USA.

Building a closer relationship with someone you love

Whether you want to build a closer relationship with a child, spouse or friend, these relationship-builders can help you to find ways to express your care for them in a meaningful way.

Remember the other person, even when you're apart. Send messages in different ways; or find a tiny gift for the person you love. Carry a photo, or something special from him/her, with you.

Enter into the emotional world of the other person and see things from his/her perspective. Be happy when s/he is happy and be sad when s/he is sad.

Love people just the way they are, accepting them without expectation of change, and offering your love and acceptance even when they make mistakes.

Appreciate and thank him/her for the special things done for you. Appreciate your relationship as well, and find ways of showing how you value the relationship.

Togetherness is vital in a healthy and growing relationship. Do the everyday things together, and spend enjoyable time together, too.

Inspire and encourage your special people to reach their goals, especially when they are feeling overwhelmed or tired.

Open yourself up and be vulnerable. Share your hopes, dreams and struggles, and encourage others to share theirs, as you listen attentively.

Needs. Understand the things that others need in relationships and know that these things may be different from the things you need. Find ways to meet each others' needs.

Support your special people when they are facing challenges. Take some of the burden from their shoulders, and be there for them at all times.

Happiness comes from making other people happy. Find new and creative ways to delight them.

Inspire your loved ones with God's love, shown through you.

Protect them from harm. Help them to feel safe from physical threats, keep their secrets, and avoid causing them extra stress or fear. Pray specifically for them whenever you can.

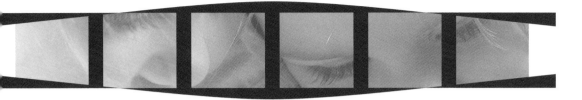

Chapter 2
Parenting for life

Love — the basis for good parenting

One of the best gifts we can give our children is our own love. This is a gift any parent can afford. Expressing love to our children is the basis for all good parenting. Children who know how much their parents love them can relate much more easily to a God who loves them. We teach children about God's love in the way we show our love to them.

We love our children, but perhaps we don't express our love as often as we need to. You can never tell a child 'I love you' too often, so do it whenever you have an opportunity! Children who feel loved are happy and healthy children. They will have less stress, and will cope with life's challenges better. They are more likely to be happier teenagers, and well-adjusted adults, healthy in body, soul and mind.

If we didn't feel loved as children, we may find it harder to express love to our own children. If this is your experience, practise with smaller expressions of love at first and add more as you grow in confidence.

Here are a few starters for you:
- I'm so glad I'm your mum/dad!
- I couldn't imagine having a more wonderful son/daughter than you!
- I have a whole hour to spend with you, what would you like to do?
- I'm so proud of you!
- Nothing you could ever do would stop me loving you!
- When God gave you to me it showed me just how much he loves me.
- I really appreciate the way you did that.
- Thank you for helping me.
- You are really great at . . . !
- I wish I could do . . . the way you do it.
- You are such a wonderful gift from God!
- Nothing is as important to me as being your mum/dad.

- You are such a special person!
- Find a way, every day, to tell your children that you love them.
- Love unconditionally, and even irrationally at times. Always let your children know they are loved by you, no matter what they do.
- Let your children know they are special and unique – help each child to discover at least one thing s/he is really good at, and do all you can to help him/her develop in that area.
- Hug your children daily. Children need physical affection from their parents in order to feel loved. Children who are starved of physical affection will often look for physical affection outside the home, especially as teenagers.
- Touch your children lovingly and gently, whenever you can. A pat on the back, a stroke on the hand, a kiss on the cheek, and even a tickle can all show children that you love and accept them.
- Send your child a card just to say, 'I love you'.
- Put a small treat in their lunch boxes or school bags.
- Write them love letters. Perhaps you could do this for every birthday.
- When you have to be away, leave or send a card saying how much you will miss them.
- Write 'I love you because . . . ' and list at least twenty different special things about your child. Give the list to your child.
- Keep their photos in your wallet and on your desk.
- Display their artwork in a special place.
- Be there at the important events in their lives, concerts, sporting events, presentations, exam times, etc.
- Forgive them freely.

The importance of listening

The gift of taking the time to listen to another person is a very precious gift. Too often people are too busy to take the time to listen to someone else. Or they are so busy thinking about what they'll say next, that they don't really listen to what is being said to them.

- When we listen to people it gives them the message that we care about them and that they are important to us.
- Listening helps us to grow closer to other people as we learn more about them.

If we don't bother to listen, if we keep interrupting our children, or if their noisy chatter makes us angry, our children will stop talking to us, and we'll close an important door into their world.

Listening is the key to a healthy relationship with our children; it's the key to understanding our children and their needs.

what they have to say.

- If you find it hard to listen, write down what is being said to you, or draw a diagram of

> **If we listen to a child when he's seven, he may still be talking and listening to us when he's seventeen!**

the information you are hearing, and ask the child if you've got it right.

- We show we're listening well when we ask thoughtful questions about what has been said.
- Wise parents listen well, and listen first, before jumping to conclusions.
- Find the time to listen to each of your children every day. Often children want to talk at bedtime.
- When your child has told you something that was very difficult for them to say, show loving encouragement and understanding rather than anger and frustration.
- Remember – if we don't take the time to listen to our children today, tomorrow they may not find the time to listen to us.

- By listening carefully we can discover what the other person's needs and concerns are, so we can offer better help and support.
- Listening helps us to understand how the other person is thinking, and what his/her interests and beliefs are.
- Listening is about respect. When we are good listeners we give the message that the person who is speaking is important to us. Even though our children may be young, and say childish things, we still need to show them respect by listening to

How well have you listened to your child recently?

See if you can answer these questions, then check your answers with your children, being careful to listen to what they have to say.

Can you name three of your children's best friends?

_____

_____

_____

What is your child's favourite subject at school?

_____

_____

What is your child's least favourite subject?

_____

_____

What do you do that annoys your children the most?

_____

_____

What would your child most like to do with you if you had a free day together?

_____

_____

What challenges are your children facing at the moment?

_____

_____

What do your children want to do when they leave school?

_____

_____

> 'My dear brothers, take note of this: Everyone should be quick to listen, slow to speak and slow to become angry.'
> James 1:19.

> 'He who answers before listening – that is his folly and his shame.'
> Proverbs 18:13.

> 'The first duty of love is to listen.' Paul Tillich.

A recipe for a good listener

1 Take one chair, sit on it and look comfortable.
2 Take one mind, and empty it of all of your own worries and thoughts. (You can always have them back later if you still want them.)
3 Take two pairs of ears, and one mouth, and use your ears twice as much as your mouth!
4 Take one child with something to say, and concentrate completely on him or her.
5 Add plenty of looking into each other's faces, together with a few hugs and hand touches, according to taste.
6 Stir gently.
7 Test every few minutes, checking that you've got the right message. Offer encouragement to tell you more.
8 Look carefully at the child's body language, and listen for repeated messages and ideas in the conversation. Respond to these with interest.
9 Serve with plenty of positive and loving responses, and decorate with smiles!

Talking so they'll listen

Communicating effectively with your child

- Use words that you know the child understands.
- Speak at the level of the child. If someone is sitting, sit to speak with him; if a child is playing in the floor, sit on the floor to speak to him. Look at the child and let him see your face as this will help him to listen to you.
- If you ask a child to do something, ask him to repeat what you've said to check that he has clearly understood your instructions.
- Use shorter sentences with small children, as longer ones can be confusing.
- Talk to your children about what you are doing and why. Explain things to them, and teach them as you do your everyday chores.
- Keep your promises to your children. If you absolutely have to break a promise, explain everything, apologise, and be sure to make another appointment. Broken promises and disappointments can undermine a child's sense of personal value and security.
- Be ready to say sorry to your child when you have made a mistake or done something to hurt him or her. If you want your child to be able to say sorry, you need to be able to model this behaviour.

Children know when parents have made a mistake and an apology will gain their respect.

- If you or your child is upset or angry, wait until everyone feels calmer before talking about something important. Sitting down in a comfortable place with a refreshing drink together makes it much easier to talk calmly.
- When a child has been courageous enough to tell the truth, reward her with love and appreciation for her honesty. Don't let your response to her give her the idea that it would have been better to lie to you. Some families choose to reduce the punishment when the child has been honest.
- Be ready to forgive your child if he or she has made a mistake.
- When your child has done something well, don't be afraid to offer praise and encouragement.
- Speaking is only a small part of communication. Our body language, facial expression and tone of voice have a much larger part to play in what we actually communicate to others. When you are talking, make sure that you are communicating well with your whole face and body.

Words are powerful

A parent's words are very powerful in helping a child to develop. Use your words to build up rather than to tear down.

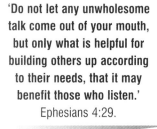

- ✓ Praise and appreciation have a much greater power for changing behaviour in a positive way.
- ✗ Nagging and criticism often lead to resentment and rebellion and don't usually bring about the positive changes we're looking for as parents.
- ✓ When we offer someone praise for doing something right, it can encourage.

'Do not let any unwholesome talk come out of your mouth, but only what is helpful for building others up according to their needs, that it may benefit those who listen.'
Ephesians 4:29.

When we offer criticism, it can discourage.

- ✓ Watch for when your children are doing something well, and praise them. Often we only comment on the things that aren't right, and we forget that most children are doing some things right most of the time!
- ✓ Praise effort as well as achievement. Some children try very hard, and still make mistakes. They need to know that it was worth all that effort, or they may give up trying altogether.
- ✓ Every day look for something to appreciate about your children, and thank or praise them for something they have done.
- ✓ Remember that a child needs a minimum of ten positive and encouraging comments for each negative comment you might make. Find as many ways as possible to encourage your children and say positive things to them.

Don't let your child grow up thinking that the only way to get your attention is to do something wrong.

If you want to destroy a child, use criticism, scolding and nagging words.
If you want to build up a child, use loving, accepting and encouraging words.

Guiding our children towards good behaviour

Setting limits for our children

Five-year-old Christopher loved football, and one day his dad took him to a real game. They arrived early and found their place in the stands. Then Dad took Christopher by the hand and said, 'Son, if you need to run around during the game, you can go along our row of seats to the steps. Then you can run up and down the steps, watching carefully to make sure no one is in your way. But you mustn't go any further than the bottom step, because then you might be in the way of the people in charge of the game.' Just to be sure, Dad took him down the stairs and showed him the bottom step, so there wouldn't be any doubt about how far Christopher could run.

Boundaries and limits are very important. If we put a fence around our land we do it to show people which piece of land belongs to us, to protect our family and belongings from trespassers and wild animals, and to protect our children and livestock from wandering away from us and into danger.

When Dad set a limit for Christopher, he did so to protect Christopher from

> **'I thank my God every time I remember you.'**
> Philippians 1:3.

having an accident, or being embarrassed. The limit was also there to protect the football game from being interrupted. It was a fair limit. It still allowed Christopher the space a young boy needs to run around from time to time.

But, as soon as the game started, Christopher ran down to the bottom step to see what his dad would do. How important was this boundary? What would happen if he got close to the limit? What action would his dad take?

As soon as his dad saw Christopher on the bottom step, he realised that his son was testing the limit. He rose from his seat and strode down the stairs. On the bottom step he sat down and held Christopher, showing him how busy the men were who ran up and down the side of the football pitch, and how Christopher could be hurt, or spoil the game if he stepped down from the bottom step. Then they held hands and walked back up the steps to their seats. Now Christopher knew that his dad meant what he said, that the limit was there to help keep him safe, and that his dad was loving and trustworthy.

How to set good limits for your child

Explain the limit clearly and check it has been understood

- Tell the child what *can* be done, rather than what can't be done. 'Stay inside the fence' is a clearer instruction for a child than 'don't go outside the fence.'
- Children tend not to hear the 'don't' part of an instruction, so rewording an instruction can make it easier for them.
- Always check that they have understood important instructions. Ask them to repeat back to you what you have said so that you are sure they have heard you and know exactly what you mean.
- Older children can be involved in the process of deciding where their limits need to be.

Give simple reasons for setting the limit

- It's easier for children to stay within the limits if the parent offers a helpful reason for the instruction.
- A parent might say, 'Only play in the garden.' But if the child knows that the limit has been put there to keep him safe and happy, then he is more likely to obey the instruction, and less likely to rebel against it.

Warn children when they are getting close to the limits

- Warn a child gently when he is getting close to the limits, in case he hasn't noticed how close he is. Try whispering a warning to him instead of shouting at him, and he may be more likely to respond positively.

What happens when a limit has been overstepped?

How did the child cross the limit?

- Is the child old enough to understand the limit? It's not very helpful to tell a 1-year-old child not to go near the steps, if he doesn't really know what steps are, or what happens if you fall down them. It's better to put up a barrier to stop the child going near the steps. If a child is too young to understand the limit, the discipline won't make any sense to him at all. If he falls down the steps and hurts himself, and then receives a spanking from an angry parent, instead of the comfort he needs, he may become frightened and confused.
- Is the child's body skilled enough to stay within the limit? Small children will spill and drop things, because they are still learning how to manage their own limbs, and they

Children need to be told what they **can** do, not just what they **can't** do!

Children who are disciplined with violence, will learn to be violent.

Children who are disciplined with love, will learn how to love.

don't understand things like gravity, or what happens when they knock over a cup of water. Accidents happen, often because we haven't arranged the environment in a very child-friendly way. When a child spills something accidentally, respond just the way you would treat your boss if he came to dinner and spilled his drink!

- Did the parent contribute to the child's behaviour by being inconsiderate of the child's needs? Children get tired and hungry and thirsty. If too much is happening around them they may become over-stimulated and miserable. If a parent is busy, a child may do something unusual, or even 'naughty' to attract the parent's attention. Before punishing a child, consider how you might have prevented the behaviour, or even how you might have contributed to the behaviour. Apologise to the child, if necessary, and take care of the immediate need.

- Did the child cross the limit deliberately to challenge you? This is the action that needs careful discipline and handling.

Teach your children good moral behaviour. The Ten Commandments are an excellent basis for good moral teaching. Give positive reasons for moral behaviour, basing your reasons on the overriding principles of loving God, loving other people, and loving yourself as well.

Discipline must be:

- prayerful – pray for yourself and your child as you consider the discipline required. God can do so much for our children that we can't always do ourselves.
- explained clearly and calmly so that it is understood by the child.
- in proportion to the mistake.
- realistic – the natural consequences of their actions are often the best learning experiences for children. Natural consequences are not a punishment; they are to help a child understand that he has choices and that those choices have consequences. Ultimately, using natural consequences leads to self-discipline and increased responsibility.
- creative – it may be easy to resort to a good spanking, because that's what you experienced as a child. But there are

many other ways to discipline a child without physical punishment. Creative discipline takes thought, but it is much more effective in the long-term.

- appropriate for the age of the child.
- kept short, so it can be put behind the child and *not be brought up again in the future*. Tomorrow is a new day with a fresh start.
- decided with the child. Children can be involved in working out what the consequences of their actions are going to be.
- consistent – children need to know that parents say what they mean.
- private – if you need to discipline your child, do so privately, and avoid doing so in front of his brothers and sisters. Children love to gloat over the punishment of others.
- balanced by an expression of forgiveness, and the reconciliation of the child with the parents.
- grace-filled – occasionally parents can take the punishment for the child, to set a Christ-like example, and to help the children understand what Jesus did for them, too.

Physical punishment is about controlling your children through fear. But 'there is no fear in love. But perfect love drives out fear, because fear has to do with punishment. The one who fears is not made perfect in love.' 1 John 4:18.

'Fathers [and mothers], do not embitter your children, or they will become discouraged.' Colossians 3:21.

Seen on a teenager's badge, 'I'm bored; forbid me to do something!'

Using natural consequences to guide a child

- When a parent sets limits for a child, the child has a choice. He can live within those limits or over-step them.
- The limits have been set to help keep the child safe and happy, and to help the family to function smoothly.
- When a child chooses to behave outside these limits, there are natural consequences. As parents, we may often feel like we want to protect our children from the natural consequences, but letting a child live with his choices can be the best way to help him learn.
- If a child stays up too late playing, is tired the next morning and is running late for school, he may need to be allowed to be late for school one day, and bear the consequences. If the parent drives him to school so that he won't be late, the child learns that it doesn't matter if he stays up late. In fact it might result in his getting a lift to school, rather than having to walk!
- If an older child doesn't come home in time to eat supper with the family, he or she needs to make his or her own food, rather than expect the family to delay their meal.
- If a child breaks something on purpose, and you know it's not

an accident, the natural consequence is that he needs to help repair the damage, or pay towards the cost.

- Physical punishment doesn't encourage children to mature and become responsible. It may teach them to conform out of fear, or to lie to avoid the punishment, or the child may become resentful.
- Using natural consequences stresses that the child needs to take responsibility for his or her own actions. Physical punishment places control in the hands of the parents, and doesn't encourage the child to consider the practical consequences.

Crazy conflicts

You've had a bad day at work. The journey home was terrible, and when you arrive at the front door you realise that you've forgotten to bring home the bread for supper. As you walk into the house, all four children are having a fight over a tennis ball. The room looks as if it has been hit by a tornado. A chair has been overturned, schoolbooks are all over the floor and a cup of water has been spilt on the table!

Your emotional temperature is in the danger range! Most parents in this situation would start to yell, or at least raise their voices a little, if only to be heard! You may want to stop the fight in case someone gets hurt, but now is probably not the best time to enter into a conflict with your children, even though it would be so easy to join the battleground with the rest of the family!

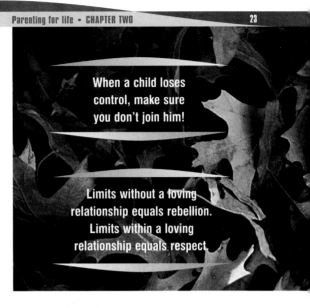

When a child loses control, make sure you don't join him!

Limits without a loving relationship equals rebellion. Limits within a loving relationship equals respect.

7 Steps to handling conflicts

1 Try to anticipate a conflict before it happens.

2 Think about your usual response to a conflict, and consider whether or not this is an effective way to handle the situation.

3 Before getting into a conflict with a child, check whether your own emotions are under control. Wait until you are both calm before entering the battleground! If you think you are not ready to face the conflict calmly, promise the child you'll talk when you are both more relaxed.

4 Give your child the space to calm down, too.

5 Have a few tasks you can do when you are feeling angry, so that you can get rid of the extra emotional energy and begin to feel calm. Clean the floors, dig the garden, go for a brisk walk, cool yourself down with a long, slow drink, or even blow a few children's bubbles!

6 Remember that it is normal and healthy for children to disagree with their parents from time to time, and to have their own opinions.

7 Conflicts are not the problem; it's how we handle the conflict that matters.

When there is a conflict we have three choices:

Choice	Consequence
1 Have a battle and fight it out together.	Having a battle usually does more harm than good and people usually get hurt, or say and do things that they regret later.
2 Surrender and give in, to avoid a conflict.	Giving in isn't very helpful because children will soon learn that you will do anything they want you to do, in order to keep the peace.
3 Have a peace-talk and work out a solution to the problem.	The best way is to sit down when you are both calm and discuss the situation. • Listen to what the child has to say first, encouraging him/her to share thoughts, feelings and concerns. • Respond lovingly, calmly stating *your* feelings and concerns. • Work together to find a solution, remembering that both sides may need to be flexible.

Conflict control
- Use words to build up rather than tear down the other person.
- Deal with one issue at a time.
- Decide how important the issue really is.
- Think about what the other person needs, and not just what you want to get out of the situation.
- Be willing to be flexible.
- Remember to say sorry.
- Remember to forgive.

Make a new start

Whenever there has been a conflict in the home, it's important to come back together again, and do everything possible to make peace, offer forgiveness, and make a fresh start. When this doesn't happen, hurt grows into resentment, communication breaks down, and it is as if a wall is being built between family members.

Red Alert!
As parents we will have those occasional days when we are stressed, anxious, tired, or ill. It's much easier for us to lose control when we're having a difficult day. Paula wears a red scarf on those days to let her children know she's not coping so well. This helps the children to be more considerate, to play more quietly, and to be more helpful.

Break down the walls

Parents have the responsibility to stop the wall being built, and to make sure that hurts are healed. If we know we've made a mistake, we need to say sorry. If the child has made a mistake, we need to offer forgiveness, and to make sure that they know how much we still love them.

Thinking about it

Following are the things that parents and children have most conflicts about.
How important will they be in a year's time? Here are some ideas to help manage conflict areas constructively.

Yelling

Yelling isn't more effective; it's just noisier and makes you look foolish!

Rather than shouting at your child, go up close and gently whisper your instructions. It can make a world of difference to how your child responds!

Untidy rooms

- Most children eventually learn how to keep their things organised by the time they have grown up.
- Some children need to be taught how to tidy their rooms and you may need to do this with them several times, and show them how to have a place for everything, to make being tidy easier.

Forgetting to clean teeth or other routine tasks

- Rather than nag children, stick signs on mirrors or doors to remind children to do routine tasks.
- Use a simple chart so that the children can tick when they have done something listed on the chart, such as packing their lunches or cleaning their shoes.
- If they forget something, whisper a gentle reminder!
- Children lived for centuries before toothpaste and toothbrushes, and it's not the end of the world if they forget once in a while!

Not eating food properly

- Parents often worry about children getting the right nutrition.
- Have set meal times and try to serve meals regularly.
- Avoid letting children eat between meals.
- Make nutritious food look attractive and taste good. Involve the children in making it.
- Praise children when they show good manners, rather than criticising them when they forget.
- Have secret codes to remind children in public of different table manners so that you do not have to draw public attention to their behaviour.

Fighting with their siblings

- The only way to prevent this is to have only one child!
- Some gentle fighting can help the children learn to defend themselves.
- Avoid comparing the children with each other, or doing anything that will encourage them to compete with each other.
- Fighting usually happens when children are bored, or want attention from their parents. Keep children busy and active and make sure that you give them the individual attention they need.
- Find tasks for them to do during which they have to co-operate, such as working together to make a special meal or celebration for the family.

Amazing Grace

Every now and then do something amazing and unexpected for your children to show them how much you love them!

Ben had a job in the school holidays, watching goats for a farmer. One day he fell asleep in the hot sun, and when he woke up, one of the goats was missing. Ben panicked. The farmer was a hard man. If he had to pay for a new goat, it would take all of his earnings. When he returned to the farm that evening the farmer told him to go and look for the goat and not come back to work until it was found.

Ben went home very worried. He told his dad about the lost goat. 'Stay here, son,' his dad said, 'I'll go in your place.' Dad took a torch and went out to look for the goat. He searched long into the night. He fell and cut his legs, and his hands were scratched and bleeding, but he kept looking until he found the goat.

The next morning Ben was amazed! Not only had his dad found the goat, but, more importantly, when he saw his dad's cuts and scratches, Ben knew just how much his father loved him.

There's a place for discipline, but there are times when our overwhelming love is the most powerful tool we have to transform our children.

blew everywhere, so Oliver stopped to help him and to apologise.

The man was very angry. 'You stupid boy!' he yelled. 'Can't you do anything right? Every time I see you you're doing something wrong! You're rude and thoughtless and you'll never be a great man like your father! He must be so disappointed in you!'

Oliver's good feelings disappeared. He hadn't meant to bump into the man; it was an accident. But listening to his angry words had destroyed Oliver's happy world.

Fortunately for Oliver he had caring parents and a teacher who understood the need for children and adults to feel happy about who they are, and their love and encouragement soon gave him back his joy and confidence.

How do you feel about yourself?
There are so many things that make us feel bad about ourselves. Some things we can't change, like our face, or our height. But many of our negative messages seem to come from the way other people treat us and talk to us. Even if these messages aren't true, and are unfair, the words still seem to roll around inside our heads, affecting us for years, if not a lifetime.

How do your children feel about themselves?
Being able to feel good about ourselves gives us dignity, self-worth, self-respect, self-confidence and a sense of peace and happiness in our lives. When we don't feel good about ourselves we tend to feel insecure, afraid, and lacking in confidence.

Most of our feelings about who we are come from our childhood experiences. If a child

Helping children feel good about themselves

Oliver's Day
Oliver felt good about himself. His mum had given him a hug that morning, before he went to school. His dad had asked for some help with the animals, and it was a big job. He helped his dad bring in an injured animal and to hold it while his dad tried to fix its wounds. Dad had thanked him for being able to help. His teacher at school had given him a good mark for his mathematics, and he even scored a goal when he played football with his friends.

Oliver was running home, full of good feelings, when he bumped into a neighbour. The man dropped his bags and his papers grows up feeling bad about himself, he probably won't feel good about himself when he's an adult, either. And he may not feel good about others.

Children who feel accepted and loved are usually:

- more confident than other children
- more able to stand up for what they believe to be right
- more able to say no when their friends try to persuade them to do harmful and dangerous things
- more able to make better friendships with others
- more healthy, physically, spiritually and emotionally
- more likely to do well at school
- more likely to be happy and less likely to suffer from depression and mental illnesses
- more likely to be successful as adults
- better able to treat others with the respect and love that they experienced as a child.

Whole communities benefit when children are brought up with these positive experiences. There is better health, less crime, more creativity and excellence in every area of life;

more caring for one another's needs and more shared happiness.

Building stronger children

We can do this with 5 building blocks:
- by seeing them as God sees them
- by spending time with them
- by the way we speak to them
- by our attitude towards them
- by our actions.

Seeing your children through God's eyes

God has placed a special value on each one of us. 'You were bought at a price.' 1 Corinthians 6:20.

- He created us and made us who we are to fit into his special plan for the world. 'For we are God's workmanship, created in Christ Jesus to do good works, which God prepared in advance for us to do.' Ephesians 2:10.
- He sent his only Son to die for us, and save us from our sins. 'But because of his great love for us, God, who is rich in mercy, made us alive with Christ even when we were dead in transgressions – it is by grace you have been saved.' Ephesians 2:4, 5.
- He is coming back to take us to heaven. 'And if I go and prepare a place for you, I will come

back and take you to be with me that you also may be where I am.' John 14:3.

- He has done everything he could to show us how much he loves us.
- The love that God has for you is the same overwhelming love he has for your children. You have the special task of helping your children to know how much God loves and treasures them. They are precious because that's what God thinks about them.

Time

- Spending time with our children is a vital part of showing them that they are valuable to us.
- If a child keeps coming to see you and you're always too busy to be bothered with him, he will soon think you are not interested in him, even if it's not true.
- Take your children with you on errands, do your chores with them, play with them, and make sure that each child has a regular time with you on her own, doing something that she wants to do.
- Working with your children also gives them the chance to build their self-confidence as they learn from watching and helping you.
- Ask them what they'd like to do with you if they had a few minutes, an hour, an evening, or even a whole day alone with

you! You might not always have lots of time, but you can make the best use of the time that you do have by doing things that are meaningful to each child.

- Even if you're often away from home, you can use the time when you are at home wisely and well.

Talk

- The way we talk to our children has one of the deepest effects on their feelings of self-worth. This is because the words that we say that hurt our children may stay in their minds and reverberate for years, even if we've forgotten the words we used, or didn't really mean to sound so harsh.
- Be very careful not to say destructive words as Oliver's neighbour did. These are words like,

God loves each one of us as if there were only one of us.

'You're so stupid', 'If only you hadn't been born', 'You'll never do anything right', and 'I'm so disappointed in you.' Replace these words with appreciative comments for what they do right, and thankful words about having them as a child in your family, such as, 'I'm so glad you're our child! If I could have put together a child myself, I'd never have made one as good as you', and 'our family is more special because you're in it!'

- Sometimes children may be naturally more hesitant and shy, and need more reassurance. Talk to them about their shy feelings, and how they can cope with difficult situations, and show that you understand their feelings.
- Ask your child for his or her

> **Whenever one person is stronger, the whole community is strengthened.**

> **The wise parent is also a bit 'short-sighted' and doesn't notice all the little mistakes a child has made, only the willing heart and the smiling face of the child who has tried so hard to please them!**

opinions about something that you may be buying, or choosing, and listen to what they have to say. Asking your children for their opinion is a good way to show respect for them, and shows that you value what they have to say.

- Remind your child that it's often those who seem the most confident that are often the most insecure, and they're acting how they would like to feel, even though inside they may feel bad about themselves.
- Praise your children when you can, especially when they've shown thoughtfulness and creativity, and have done their best, even if it's not completely perfect!
- So many parents are afraid to appreciate and encourage their children in case it will make them proud, but, by *not* doing so, they may make their children weak and insecure. Appreciation doesn't make a child proud; it can make him strong.

Attitudes

- Have a thankful attitude towards your children, for who they are as well as what they do.
- Look for the best in your children, and show appreciation for what you see.
- Smile! A parent's smile can be the sunshine for a child's entire day!
- Keep in mind the message that this child is wonderful because he or she is *your* child.
- Even if your child is far from perfect, keep on believing the best and acting on that belief. It will do far more good for your child than listening to nagging and criticism!

> Call a child a fool and he'll be a fool. Call him great and he'll be great.

Actions

- Hugs, pats on the back, and gentle touches can all help children to feel good about themselves.
- Giving children responsibilities that they can handle also boosts their self-worth and confidence, because it shows them that they are trustworthy.
- When they do make mistakes, come alongside gently and help them quietly pick up the pieces.

Thinking about it

- Think back to your own childhood.
- Are there any words your parents said that still resound loudly in your mind and bother you?
- Are there messages your parents gave you that help and encourage you? What has it been like to live with those messages?
- What messages would you like to have recorded in your own children's minds, to help them through the challenges of life?
- Lots of adults carry heavy burdens of bad feelings too. Even though you can't go back in time and change their childhoods, you can still use some of these ideas to encourage someone who is struggling as an adult.
- Reach out and strengthen someone today.

Preparing your child for life

The ultimate goal of parenting is to launch our children into life, as fully-equipped as possible. It can be easy to forget this goal when they are small. But even when they are little, we can begin to guide them in the right direction.

How to help your child journey into adulthood:

- From the time he is born, learn how to see every child as a gift from God, and a person to be nurtured into a happy and healthy adult life.
- At each stage of development find ways to increase personal independence within safe boundaries.
- Being independent is not the only goal we have for our children; they also need to learn to live as part of a family, and as part of a community, and we need to teach children how to be

*inter*dependent with others, too.
- Allow your children to make mistakes at times, so they can learn about consequences to actions and choices.
- Be ready to listen to your children, whatever they have to say. Accept their concerns and feelings rather than reacting against what they are thinking and doing.
- Be there to talk to them about the important issues in life, such as sexuality and relationships, life, death, and faith. Children need to hear these things from you first.
- Keep in touch with their peer culture and the current issues.
- Make it your goal to stay friends with your children at all times. Remember that we change people more by love and appreciation, than we do by criticism, rejection and nagging.

Life-skills to teach to your children:

- How to have a strong faith in a loving and merciful God.
- How to behave politely and develop good social skills.
- How to be considerate and appreciative of others.
- How to manage their anger appropriately.
- How to listen to other people effectively.
- How to have a positive and cheerful approach to life.
- How to find happiness in doing things for others.
- How to keep themselves and those around them safe from harm and danger.
- How to take care of their bodies, with good hygiene, healthcare, diet, exercise, sleep,

water and fresh air.
- How to express gratitude to God and to those around them.
- How to do a job well.
- How to start a task and see it through to completion.
- How to manage money wisely.
- How to find help when they are lost, in danger, or in difficulty.
- How to cook a simple meal, clean a house and do the laundry.
- How to stay safe from drugs, premarital sex, alcohol, and violence.
- How to do simple household repairs safely.
- How to do one thing so well that they could use the skill to earn money if ever they needed to, such as driving, teaching music lessons, crafts and sewing skills, child-care, gardening, etc.
- How to do anything else that you consider to be an important life skill in your home and community.

Teach your children:
- By your own example.
- By treating them the way you would like them to treat others.
- By explaining simply what you are doing and why.
- By being willing to live with their mistakes during the learning process.
- By letting them work alongside you.
- By letting them take on more of the task when they feel confident to do so.
- By having a life-long learning attitude to life (no matter how old I am I can still learn).
- By appreciating their effort even when they don't always do things right.
- By encouraging them to learn useful skills that are being taught in the community.

Thinking about it:
- Make a plan for each of your children.
- List the specific skills they will need to live successfully as adults in your community.
- Think about the things each child can already do, and show him appreciation for what he has learned and achieved.
- Think about the things they still need to practise, or learn, and think how you will take steps to help them develop those skills, according to their age and ability.
- Talk with older children about what they would like to achieve, and set goals together. Ask them about the best way to help them learn the things they need to know, and take their preferences into consideration.
- Fill out a piece of paper like the diagram over and use it to help guide your plans and discussion.
- Review your plans for each child, and yourself, regularly.

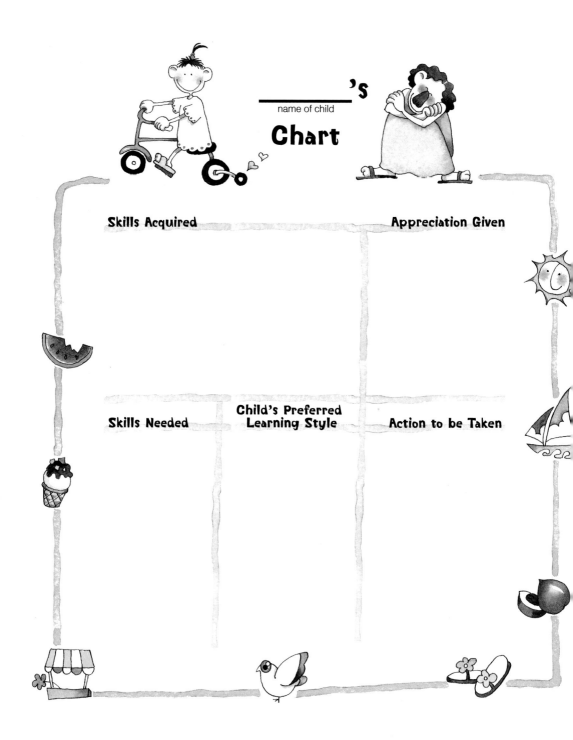

_____'s
name of child

Chart

Skills Acquired

Appreciation Given

Skills Needed

Child's Preferred Learning Style

Action to be Taken

'Train a child in the way he should go, and when he is old he will not turn from it.' Proverbs 22:6.

Helping children to make wise choices

Most of our lives are made up of countless different choices about what we eat, where we go, who our friends are, what we choose to say, what we choose to do, and even what we choose not to do. In one day a human being could be faced with hundreds or even thousands of choices, big and small. Sometimes our happiness, and even our very lives, can depend upon the choices we've made. So it's a good idea to help children learn how to make the right choices when they're young.

Home is a safe place to begin making choices when you are a child. The choices are usually about small things, and if you make a wrong choice it's less embarrassing, and your parents are there to support you. As a parent it's often easier to make a choice for a child, rather than let him do it for himself. It's much quicker to give a child a shirt and tell him to put in on, than ask him what he wants to wear and wait for him to decide. But wise parents can help their children develop good choice-making skills.

Learning to choose
- When children are young, start by giving them a limited choice, such as between two different, and visible objects, and slowly increase the range of choices.
- One of the first things they will learn is that when they make one choice, it usually means they can't have the alternative too. This can be a difficult concept for a very young child, but it's an important part of making decisions that needs to be learned. This can start from learning that they can't eat their dinner out of two bowls. If they choose a red bowl, then they can't have the blue bowl.

- As children grow older they may need to realise that if they buy a red shirt, there's not enough money for a blue shirt too; they can have one or the other. On a more serious level, when they grow older, they will have learned that if they choose one wife, they have to exclude others.
- When children learn that making one choice excludes another, they learn to value their choices and consider more thoughtfully the different options and outcomes.
- Help children make good choices by giving them positive options. 'I have to go to town for a day, so you can stay with Grandma, go to work with Dad, or stay with your friend Nicky,' rather than 'I'm going to town and you can't come, and I don't want you playing outside on the streets with Jim or Bob.' Say what their choices *are*, and not what their choices *can't be*. This gives them a clearer idea about how to make a good choice.

- Slowly, as the children grow in confidence at making their own decisions, let them make their own choices and accept the results of their choices. Sometimes it's only by letting children make an occasional unwise choice, in a safe area, that they will begin to value the importance of making wise choices.
- It's important to let a child know that you love her whatever choices she makes. She mustn't be made to feel that she is less valued or loved by you because she has made a mistake. Shelley's mum (see 'Shelley's dress') didn't get angry at her daughter, she simply stated that the dress had to last all year, and then showed her how to repair it so that the patches would show as little as possible. This taught Shelley good sewing skills to help her fix the situation. Mum involved her in repairing the dress, because it was important for Shelley to understand how much extra work was involved in an unwise choice.
- Help children to learn that their decisions often have an impact outside of their own lives. When Shelley's dress fabric wore thin, her mum had to give up extra time to help her fix her dress. It wasn't only Shelley who had to bear the consequences of her choice. Sometimes a choice that one person makes will affect the whole family, and it's respectful to consider how our choices will make a difference, for better or worse, in other people's lives.
- As adults you can demonstrate good decision making skills in the home. There are lots of decisions that need to be made daily. Let your children see you make choices and talk about decisions within the family so that they learn good decision-making skills from you. Talk through decisions with your spouse, and as a family. Discuss the possible results of each choice openly and calmly, letting each person have a say. Show respect for everyone's opinion, and share the responsibility for the decision that is chosen.
- Whenever a child makes a good choice, praise him, let him know that his choice was good, and tell him what was good about it. This increases the child's confidence in his own decision-making skills and encourages him to make good choices in the future. Help him to evaluate

Shelley's dress

Shelley needed a new dress for school. It had to last her for a year. Mum took her to choose some fabric and she chose some thin, pretty fabric, rather then the heavier, stronger, but less attractive fabric she usually wore. Mum agreed to buy the fabric if Shelley would wear the dress for a year. Mum then made her a lovely dress and Shelley was delighted. But the delicate fabric didn't wear so well. After a few months it began to wear thin and fray. Shelley wanted a new dress, but mum reminded her she couldn't have a new one till the end of the year. Mum helped Shelley patch and repair the dress to wear all year long, but Shelley soon learned that fabric needs to be more than just pretty to make a good dress.

'Choose for yourselves this day whom you will serve. . . . But as for me and my household, we will serve the Lord.' Joshua 24:15.

his own choices. Is there anything he would like to change about his decision? Was there anything she learned by her choice?

Important choices
There are several areas in life where making a good choice is very important. The friends they choose, the education and career they choose, and the way they spend their money are all choices that will have a great impact on children's lives and the future happiness of both themselves, and their families.

Friends
- When choosing a friend, encourage the child to consider if the person is a good or a bad influence in his life. Is the friend kind and respectful to other children and to those who are in authority, such as teachers and parents? What does the child especially like or dislike about the person, and how will that make a difference to the friendship? Are there any concerns the child has about the person? Remind the child that the way their new friend treats other people may be the way the person will treat him one day.

Schooling and careers
- Help children to make wise choices about their schooling, future and career choices. How can they discover what their strengths and talents are, and which school subjects are best suited to them, if they have a choice to make? What are the children own life goals? What jobs would they like? What steps do they need to take to reach their goals, both now and in the future? What other alternatives might there be if the

first choices don't work out? What is the importance of working hard to reach these goals?

Money
- When it comes to spending, children need to think about using their money wisely. When they make a purchase, is it necessary? Is the thing they want to buy the most important thing they need, or is there something else they have to save their money for? Will the item do the job well? Is it good value for money and will it last? Do they like it well enough to live with it for the next few years?

Decisions, decisions. It's not always easy to make the right choices, but you can help your children to make the best decisions when they need to. A little practice now may help them make the best decisions for a lifetime.

Watching what they watch

Television is a powerful tool that many of us have in our homes. It can be a useful tool, but it can also be misused. How is it used in your home?

Ask yourself:

Are you happy with the influence it has? How can you and your children use it wisely?
Is the television helping to grow the character that you would like your children to have?

USEFUL aspects of television

- There are some excellent educational programmes on television that can teach children about nature, science, history, literature and religion, stimulate their artistic creativity, or help them to learn about relationships and life in positive ways.
- It can be helpful to know that you can have a few moments space as an adult while your child watches a guaranteed safe programme or video.
- Television can open a window on the world and take the children to places you would never be able to visit as a family.

CHALLENGING aspects about television

- A television is not a good babysitter. Children need you to talk to them, and to watch what they are watching so that you can discuss your concerns and their ideas.
- Not everything that is advertised as children's television is suitable for *your* children.

Biblical Guidelines

The Bible has some good guidelines for watching television and videos, reading books and choosing computer games:

'Whatever is true, whatever is noble, whatever is right, whatever is pure, whatever is lovely, whatever is admirable – if anything is excellent or praiseworthy – think about such things.' Philippians 4:8.

Not everything you want to watch or read will fit all these categories. It can be helpful to think about the categories separately. If a programme fits into one or more categories, then it may be suitable, but only you can decide, because you know your children and your own personal standards. Things that are true may be biographies and history. Noble stories are those where high moral standards are upheld. These stories may not be true, but they can teach good principles of service, bravery, and caring for others. Stories about good principles and choices may be 'right'. Some stories and programmes are pure, lovely and innocent, but they may not be true, or even noble. Some may be praiseworthy, and win awards for good literature, but they may still not meet other standards you have. It will be up to you to decide which values are most important for you and your children.

- Children need to be children. They should not be exposed to a world of violence, adult concerns, exaggerated fictional stories that look like real life, sexual images, and even the news.
- Commercial television can encourage children to become materialistic as they see all the latest toys, clothes and food advertised in appealing ways.
- Children have different fears and interests. Many of the cartoon stories have terrifying moments, or horrible monsters that can frighten some children and give them nightmares.
- Some programmes allude to witchcraft and the supernatural, others may show children involved in activities that Christian families would not condone, or that encourage children to rebel against their parents.
- Television time is time that could be spent more productively by the child, developing his skills, having fun exercise, being creative, or relating to real people, rather than actors on a screen.
- Children may try to copy some of the things they see others do on television. Television has many role models. Make sure that your children are exposed to the positive role models and not the negative ones.

Practical things to consider

- Talk to your children about how and why it is important to choose carefully what we watch. Think about what your own reasons may be. If you don't think they should watch a certain programme, tell them why and explain your reasons.

- Make sure that the parents of your children's friends know what your television code is, or say, 'My child has nightmares whenever she sees scary things and I would like to know what videos she might watch at your house, just to make sure she'll be all right with it.'
- Know what your children are watching at their friends' homes. Talk to them about what to do if they find they are watching something they don't like, or that they know you wouldn't let them watch. One child chooses to say that he needs to go home because he isn't feeling well. Another calls with a coded message, such as, 'Is Katie coming over today?' so that the parent can come and take her home.

- Provide lots of interesting alternatives to television. Have a board games night. Involve your children in music lessons, sports, or other extra-curricular activities so that they have other things to do after school.
- You could limit television watching to a specific time. Or go through the television guide together talking about which programmes are good to watch. Put a star on the guide next to anything that you agree would be good to watch, and then don't watch anything else.
- Watch what *you* watch! Are you following good guidelines about your own television watching? Set a good example by your own choice of viewing, and the quantity of television you watch.
- Make a little sign to go on the television screen reminding the family to be careful what they watch. Perhaps the children could design and make the sign.
- You may like to avoid children having televisions in their own rooms, where you won't be able to monitor what they watch, and where they will be isolated from the rest of the family.
- If you have a video recorder, record some good programmes for the children to watch instead of the programmes you don't like.

'What can we do if we can't watch TV?'

- Learn a new sport.
- Go for a walk to the park.
- Read a classic book together.
- Cook dinner together.
- Learn a new craft skill or musical instrument.
- Play with a construction toy.
- Play a game together.
- Write your own play and act it out at a family party.
- Build a shelter indoors (or outdoors in a safe place) and eat or sleep in it.
- Do a jigsaw puzzle.
- Make a fruit salad.
- Make home-made ice cream.
- Write a story.
- Make up a puzzle for other family members to solve.
- Start an illustrated journal, adding funny stickers or your own drawings.
- Start a collection – stamps, postcards, model engines, china pigs, feathers, leaves, grasses – anything!
- Write someone a letter.
- Weed the garden.
- Tidy up the books in your room.
- Create something totally out of junk.
- Ride a bike.

Helping your child to feel comfortable with his or her gender

Harry's Daughters

Harry and his wife had six daughters. Six beautiful and healthy daughters. Harry's friends would tease him because he didn't have any sons, and they would ask him if he wouldn't rather have six sons instead. But Harry wouldn't let them tease him. 'I've got six daughters,' he'd say proudly, 'and they're worth more to me than any sons!'

'But daughters will never work as hard as our sons!' the friends would say. And Harry would answer, 'And your sons will never be as beautiful as my daughters!'

Harry was a wise father who was determined not to let the attitudes of his culture damage his relationship with his children, or let his children feel undervalued. He decided to let his daughters know that he loved them just as they were.

The daughters were strong and worked well, and he helped them find something that they were good at, so that they would always be able to work to support themselves if necessary. He taught them skills that usually only boys are taught, not so that they would be just like boys, but so that they could have confidence in fixing things for themselves, and in understanding how things worked. His friends laughed at him, but Harry knew that his daughters needed even more of his love and acceptance in a society that tended to undervalue women.

How can you be a wise parent, helping your children to feel good about who they are, and respectful of the opposite sex?
The 1 to 18 code:

1 Firstly, accept your children just as they are, whether they are a boy or a girl. Let them know that they are best being just who they are. Take special care not to let little girls think that they are not as good as boys, or that you wish they'd been born boys. As soon as they are born, children need to know that they are loved regardless of whether they are boys or girls.

2 Be gentle with their bodies, especially their genitals, and avoid doing anything that would cause them pain in that area. Clean their bodies gently when they are babies and show them how to keep their bodies clean and hygienic as they grow older, to prevent any infections and sores. Help them to understand why boys' and girls' bodies are different, and why that is special.

3 Our differences enable us to have children and to share our skills in the home. A man cannot have children without a woman, nor a woman without a man. Both have an important role to play; but in many ways the woman has the larger role when it comes to having children. It's her body that carries the unborn child, and then feeds the baby when it's born.

4 Regularly reaffirm your children for being the gender that they are. If your culture tends to value one sex above another, then you need to work harder to help your son or daughter to feel good about who s/he is. Don't let your culture pressure you into devaluing your children. When women are valued and respected, a community can be stronger. A mother who feels good about herself is more likely to nurture strong and happy children of both sexes, so if you want great sons, it's important for them to have a mother who feels valued and loved, too.

5 Teach children to value and respect the other sex. It's important for girls to respect men, and this respect usually comes from the daughter being able to respect and love her father. If she can have a good relationship with her dad, then this will help her to develop the skills to have a good relationship with her future husband.

6 Likewise, boys who have a good relationship with their mother, and love and respect her, are more likely to treat their wives with loving respect. Teaching your children to respect, love and care for other family members when they are young will help to ensure that your children have strong and happy marriages.

7 Treat boys and girls equally in the home, and avoid giving either special privileges. Share food according to age, not gender. Try to help all your children to have as good an education as possible. Educated mothers learn skills that help them to be better mothers, and they and their children are often healthier than the children of mothers with very little education.

8 Encourage the children to spend time with their same sex parent. A mother is a good model for her daughters and the father for his sons. Help them to make the most of their masculine and feminine features. Be the best men and women they can be.

9 Talk about differences in gender and show how each has special advantages. Men may be physically stronger, and able to work hard. Some men are very good at solving problems. Women are made so that they can have babies, and that is also a very special privilege. Some women enjoy their close friendships and find comfort in talking about the concerns in their life. Women's bodies are softer in shape and they have finer features.

10 Privacy and modesty can mean different things in different cultures. In some countries women must be totally covered. In other countries both men and women may wear very little. Whatever your culture, find ways to respect one another's need for privacy within the home.

11 Having a place where family members can change their clothes without being seen by others may show respect. Respect may also mean knocking at a closed door and being invited to enter, rather than opening a door without considering who may be behind the door, and whether they are doing something that they wish to do in private.

12 Tell your children ahead of time what will happen to their bodies as they grow older, and tell them how to deal with the changes. This information gives confidence to the child as he or she feels better able to manage the changes that come with growing up. Be positive about these changes and talk about them as facts.

13 Make the changes that happen as their bodies mature something to look forward to and not to fear. Give them accurate medical information about their bodies, and not folklore. If you're not sure what is really true, ask a doctor or nurse to help you know what to say.

14 If you were given information by your parents that was inaccurate or unhelpful, then give better information to your children. Tell the facts instead, and use words that will encourage your children and help them to be proud of their maturing bodies.

15 Teach your children how to keep their bodies safe. Teach them what is acceptable sexual behaviour and what is not acceptable sexually, and teach them how to avoid being sexually abused. Let your children know that their genitals are private and not for others to touch and see. Teach the children that if someone is interested in touching and seeing their private places, then they should run away from the person and tell you what happened, even if the person is an adult they trust, or a friend.

16 It is especially important to protect girls from being molested and raped. Do all you can to ensure their safety at all times, and to teach them how to avoid situations where they could be harmed.

17 Make sure that your children understand about illnesses that are passed between people sexually, especially the HIV virus and AIDS. The best time and place for the first sexual encounter is in a secure and married relationship. This

protects everyone against the spread of disease, and keeps the community and the children healthy.

18 Think about the different ways men and women live and behave in your community and find advantages for both the genders.

Some of these ideas may seem strange to you because they may be new, and may be very different from the views expressed in your community. But think about the ideas. Even those that seem strange at first make more sense when you've thought about them for a while. The wisest people don't always follow the patterns of the past. They consider each pattern, each tradition, and decide for themselves which ideas are still helpful and good, and whether there may be some better ideas waiting to be discovered.

Emily's story

Emily wasn't happy with the way her mother treated her when she was young. She loved her mother, but couldn't understand some of the traditional ways of handling little girls, especially traditions that caused pain to their bodies. She decided that she would treat her little girls differently and not hurt them in any way. It was hard taking the decision to be different. Many people were angry with her, but as she talked with them, more and more people began to see that she was right, and that she had a better way.

Helping your children feel good about who they are is always a better way to live.

'There is neither Jew nor Greek, slave nor free, male nor female, for you are all one in Christ Jesus.' Galatians 3:28.

Creating an everyday surprise!

Having an element of surprise in daily life can create lots of humour and anticipation that can add a sparkle to your family experience.

Take a small soft toy, like a mouse, or a small monkey, and hide it in a different place every day for the children to find. Look for funny and unusual places to hide the toy, sometimes in places where the child will find it by accident (such as among their clothes, in a shoe, or in a cereal packet), and sometimes where they will have to search harder.

Occasionally have something unexpected for breakfast. Remember that this is only an occasional treat, and let them have ice cream on their cereal, breakfast in bed, dessert before dinner, a meal in a place where you don't normally eat, or an indoor picnic on the floor of their room.

Let the children experiment and create amazing fruit cocktails from various fruit juices, or 'smoothies' where soft fruits are blended together with an electric blender, and mixed with a little juice or yoghurt to create a delicious and healthy drink. Serve in attractive glasses with drinking straws.

Have a pink day when everyone wears at least something pink (or whatever other colour you choose). Every meal must also include the colour. Yellow, green and purple also work well, but it is hard to find blue food!

Take on someone's pet for a week if a neighbour or friend is going away, or would like a break. Find out how to look after the pet well, and take care of all its needs, and then give it back at the end of the week.

If you have family photo albums, look at them together and talk about the happy memories you have.

If you can find the right place to do so, create a safe camp fire in the evening and sit around it telling stories and singing songs.

Choose a theme for the week and let the children decorate the table or the house according to the theme. Think of activities to do around the theme, such as crafts, stories and games. This can be a helpful treat when the children are not at school.

Fill a box with things like string, safe scissors, washable glue, coloured card and paper, pipe cleaners, fabric oddments, beads, feathers, etc. Let the children use the things in the box to make anything they like, or give them a theme such as making a bird, a birthday card, or a flower. Top this box up with unusual and interesting packaging, bubble wrap, foil, etc, and use it to stimulate your child's creativity.

'A cheerful look brings joy to the heart, and good news gives health to the bones.'
Proverbs 15:30.

Creating special memories

An important part of having a successful family is creating special memories. Even in the most challenging times, happy memories can be created with words, creativity, imagination and family traditions.

Special memories help to create positive family stories that may be told for generations to come, and help to give the family roots and stability in an uncertain world.

There are lots of different ways to create a memory. Think about some of these ideas and then adapt them to suit your own family.

- Create individual memories not just as a family but between each parent and each child.
- Do some things routinely, such as every week on the same night, or every birthday. These can be very simple, such as lighting candles, reading a book aloud together, going for a walk to the same place, or writing a letter on each birthday. Simple things can create special memories, as well as the once-in-a-while unusual surprise!
- Going to bed routines will change as a child grows older, but even these can create memories if you develop a special way of hugging each child as you say good night. You could sing a funny song, rub noses together, create your own hand-shake, say a rhyming prayer, or offer a good-night blessing.
- Find things to celebrate. Some families are concerned about having celebrations, but God's annual calendar for the children of Israel

contained lots of celebrations, rituals and traditions. Find things to rejoice about, from the smallest event, like a child passing a spelling test, to something big like Dad getting a new job! Then plan ways to celebrate the successes and happy times in the family.

- Think of ways to make even ordinary days extraordinary.
- Try to do something unusual as a family once a month, and plan ahead so that everyone always has something to look forward to.
- Involve the children in the plans for special events. Listen to their ideas and ask for their help. Accept whatever they make and do towards the event with love and gratitude, and find a way to give their work a prominent place in the activities.
- Find lots of ways to laugh together as a family.

Ideas for developing traditions and family celebrations:
- Use the ideas and traditions that you're comfortable with from your

'A cheerful heart is good medicine.'
Proverbs 17:22.

own culture as the basis of your own family traditions. This is an important heritage to pass to your children. Help them to feel good about their background and culture.
- Often the traditions of your faith can be a source of ideas for family celebrations.
- Ask the children for ideas, and let them create some traditions of their own for the family to adopt.
- Talk to other people about their family traditions and special memories and find out what *they* do.
- Borrow books from the library, or find other ways to learn about other cultures and their traditions, and have evenings when you eat food from different cultures, learn about their celebrations, and even dress up like them.
- Think about the special memories you had as a child and try to pass these on to your children.
- Think about some of the memories you would like to have had, and see if you can make them a reality for your children.
- Write things down, take photos, or tell stories together to keep the memories that you make fresh and alive.

Family Traditions

- Do something special on your wedding anniversary, to show that marriage is important to you, and so that the children can see that their parents enjoy being married to each other. One couple invited their children to a dinner in their own home, and recreated the celebration meal on their anniversary. Mum and dad wore their wedding clothes, and served the children. They looked at wedding photos and told stories about when they were first married.

'Rejoice with those who rejoice.'
Romans 12:15.

- Create some new words for things that no other family has, and enjoy using them. You could even use the funny words that the children once used when they were little!
- Make things together. You could make a garden, build a shed, redecorate a room, or learn a new skill together.
- Prepare a meal together and eat it in an unusual place, or in an unusual way.
- Have one night a week when the children decorate the table or the place where you eat, in any way they like.
- Have some family fun days when only the necessary chores are done, and everyone is together all day, relaxing and playing together.
- Make up your own games to play.
- Light a fire outside, sit around it and sing, tell funny stories and cook simple food over the embers.
- Plant a tree each time a child is born. Take care of the tree and visit it each year with the child.
- Create simple and inexpensive gifts and treats for one another, like a bunch of wild flowers, a few favourite fruits, an unusual stone, a simple card or a letter.
- Share the funny stories about your day at each evening meal, before you talk about the challenges of your day. Read funny books together and play funny games.
- Find a catalogue or old magazine and let each person cut out pictures of the gifts they would like to give to one another, if they had an unlimited budget!

Remember that it's the thought that counts, and this can be a special activity to share together.

Think about it:

- What special memories do you have from your childhood?
- What special things would you like your children to remember about their childhood?
- What happy memories have you already created as a family?
- What memories are you planning to make with your family?

More great experiences to share with your children

- Go on an overnight camping trip together, taking all your camping gear and food with you. Light a fire, if it's safe and legal to do so, and cook your supper outdoors.
- Help your child to plan and cook a meal for everyone else in the family. Try not to use packet foods!
- Buy a science kit and do some of the experiments together.
- Learn a new sport together.
- Learn a traditional skill that is dying out in your country, to help keep it alive.
- Climb a mountain together.
- Sew a simple garment together with your daughter, letting her choose the fabric and the pattern. Look for the easy-to-sew patterns. Teach your son how to do simple mending too.
- Go to a special show, concert or ballet performance together.
- Work on a small business project together: making creative greeting cards to sell to friends, growing plants, pet-sitting, etc.

Choose a project where you already have some experience, and pass on your skills to your children.

- Teach your child how to take care of a car, change tyres, change oil, top up the radiator, wash and polish the paintwork, etc. Take an evening class in car maintenance together.
- Take an overnight mother-and-daughter, or father-and-son trip to a never-visited place, and explore it together.
- Work together to design and make something special for the home. It could be a bed cover, a cushion/pillow cover, decorating the walls, or giving some old furniture a fresh look, etc.
- Find a mission project you can work on together, from helping with the children's programme at church, and wrapping toys as presents for needy children, to building new churches in another country.
- Show your child how to mend things around the house, such as changing plugs and light bulbs, unblocking drains, drilling holes in walls, home decorating skills etc.

What teenagers wish their parents knew

by Beth Holford*

- Don't be someone you aren't in order to fit in. Don't dress differently, or use my slang. I'll just get embarrassed or annoyed.
- If you disapprove of something I'm doing, tell me once in a non-confrontational way, then leave it. I'll have gotten the message the first time.
- If you are interested in my life, ask a general question. If you get a short answer – leave it. It generally isn't anything personal; I'm just not in a talkative mood. Sometimes I'll tell you a lot – but don't press the matter.
- Linked to that point, don't try to ask my friends about my life behind my back: It's embarrassing and demeaning, and will probably stop me telling you anything in future.
- If I do want to talk, make time for me. I probably really need your support!
- Ask how I best feel loved and act accordingly. Some people like hugs; some people would rather have time, or small thoughtful acts or gifts. This doesn't mean spoiling me – just showing that you appreciate me.
- Be flexible. This works for any aspect of parenting – discipline, curfews, chores, allowances, anything. Being willing to bend rules for me occasionally shows you have your priorities right and will stop me feeling resentful.
- I don't *mind* doing chores from time to time, but put them in perspective. Make me think ahead to when I move away from home and will have to do all the cooking, washing, cleaning, ironing and maintenance for myself. Please encourage me to learn so that I can one day be independent!
- Give me more responsibility and independence as I get closer to leaving home. For example, give me an allowance for clothing instead of handing over money on demand. I'll never learn to budget otherwise.
- Don't ask my friends about their lives, don't patronise them, and don't brag about me to them! None of us will appreciate it, and we'll just try to avoid you.
- Tell me that you love me, especially after an argument. I don't know why, but it just seems to help!

- Don't take everything I say in an argument personally; hormones, etc, are running around and I will most likely be sorry later. I still love you!
- Don't relive your teenage years through me. If you push me to do something you always wished you had done, I'll either feel overly burdened to achieve or I'll be rebellious and make you feel worse.
- Understand that the main attraction of church is probably friends, so let me go to a church where there are people my age to keep me in the faith during my teen years. This isn't a sign that I have no interest in Christianity, I simply need peer support.
- Don't get so caught up in trying to win an argument that you forget the point you're trying to make, or bring up petty issues or past wrongs. That won't help your case. And when you do pick a fight, make sure it is a really worthwhile one, otherwise you might find that my moral priorities become very mixed up.
- When you're proud of me, tell me so. Encourage me whenever possible. No matter what I might say, I do value your opinion and praise.

- Don't shelter me. If you find out I'm planning to do something you are not happy about, don't forbid me to do it. State your case by all means so I know the reasons why I shouldn't do it, but if I choose, let me make my own mistakes. It'll help me learn, and I might trust you next time you give advice. But don't tell me 'I told you so'. I'll be embarrassed enough at being wrong as it is!
- On the other hand – if *you* mess up – admit it. I'm old enough to know that parents aren't perfect and I'll respect you more if you own up and apologise. (Also on this – don't try to pass the blame onto anyone else. I'll pick up on it and just feel more annoyed at you.)
- Whenever you set a rule, let's discuss the reason for it, and if necessary change it slightly. If I think it's pointless I'm likely to rebel against it, which will lead to more avoidable arguments and punishments.
- Respect me for who I am. Don't compare me with anyone else – a friend, sibling or yourself at my age. I don't need that kind of pressure. I need unconditional acceptance from you.
- If you really have to talk about something like sex, then just be blunt and open, otherwise we'll both be embarrassed. However, topics like these are generally best avoided.
- If you want to get to know me, do it on my terms. If I'm a girl, offer to take me shopping and treat me to a new outfit, or if I'm a guy maybe buy tickets for a sports match I'd like to see. This sounds like bribery, . . . actually it is, but that doesn't matter! It's an opportunity to talk and make a memory and that's the important thing.

* Beth is the teenage daughter of Karen Holford.

Time management for teens

by Sam Davis*

David remembers that when he was still in his late teens, several decades ago, it was his parents' expectation that he should be home and indoors by 10.30pm. Even when he was 18 the rule didn't change. He also remembers that this was an area of great disagreement between him and his parents, particularly him and his dad. Interestingly, when his dad came to visit the other day, and they started to talk about the curfews David had set for his own teens, Dad said that midnight was the deadline that he remembered setting for David. David quickly reminded him of the truth!

So what is a reasonable time for the modern Christian teenager to be back home at night? First of all we need to define what we're talking about and the family needs and situation. Obviously the requirements will vary according to the age of the teenager. Those who are 16 and under should, during the week, come home after school depending on distance and journey time. Reasonably speaking this should be in time for the evening meal. This allows for some after-school activities, and needs to be in agreement with the parents' wishes.

If teens wish to come home later than this during the week, they need to have parental consent, to have shown that they have made arrangements to travel home safely.

There is no doubt that we are living in far more dangerous times than ever before. It is naïve to think or argue that 'I'm OK. I can look after myself' when we hear of children and young people being abducted or going missing. It sends a chilling reminder to teens and parents alike.

When David was young he remembered that his dad would agree for him to come home later at weekends (up until midnight) if he had gone to a party or church social event, etc. On these occasions he would make arrangements to travel home safely.

To suggest to today's young people that they need to leave a party by midnight, or at least try to get home by midnight, is regarded by some as unreasonable and uncool. The truth is, many of today's youth events are starting at a time when most reasonable parents think they should be finishing! So what can a parent do?

How you manage this, and the times you set for your teens, will depend upon the youth culture and the environment where you live. This is how some parents have dealt with the situation in their own homes.

When teens stay out late

- If you are picking up your teens, plan to arrive at a time that you think is reasonable and acceptable for you both.
- Discuss this time and come to an agreement with your young person before the event. (This may not be easy because reasonable for them may be 6am next morning!)
- Recognise that they do have feelings and can be embarrassed. Listen to their concerns.
- Once you have agreed on what you both consider to be a reasonable time, stick to it.
- Don't turn up at the function at the agreed time and publicly call them out. This is not good for your teen's image. Try to get word to them discreetly that you are waiting outside. If your teen has a mobile phone, try sending a text message or something.
- Show appreciation for your teens when they leave events promptly as arranged.

- Successfully negotiating the first of such arrangements will build trust and confidence for future events.

Home is the best place for all self-respecting young people at night until they leave home. What we're doing as parents is preparing them for the day when they make that move so that they will be good and efficient managers of their time, and so that they will consider their own safety and transportation at night.

Many young people want to spend their nights out at the weekends, experiencing all sorts of entertainment, and then sleeping in most of the next day. This doesn't really prepare them for the greater responsibility of further education, marriage and the work place. The old saying 'early to bed, early to rise makes a man healthy, wealthy and wise' was a sensible one.

Those who burn the candle at both ends will find that their candle melts twice as fast!

* Sam Davis is a minister with experience in counselling.

Helping your teens to handle sexual pressure

Paul was concerned for his children. They were growing up fast. Soon they would be adults. He looked at the other children he knew who were in their teenage years, and he was sad. So many of them were exploring relationships and getting hurt. Some of the girls were already pregnant. Some had babies. Some of them had probably already contracted HIV.

Paul knew that it was much better for young people to wait until they were married before having sex, even though so many of them didn't think it was necessary to wait. Paul thought about the reasons why he had waited until he was married before having sex with his wife. He'd realised that sex wasn't just for fun; it was very serious. Sex is a matter of life and death – it can create a baby, it can give you a terminal disease, or it can cause guilt and worry. Whenever two people have sex it binds them closely together, and if the two

separate again, the hurt and emotional damage can be long lasting.

So what could Paul do to help his own teenagers make the best choices about their sexuality?
Paul thought about some of the reasons why teenagers want to try sex before they get married. They want some fun. Everyone else they know does it. They want to feel loved, accepted and attractive. They don't think about the responsibility that may be involved if sex results in pregnancy, or the horror of contracting a life-threatening disease.

Teach correct and age-appropriate material about sexuality
Firstly, Paul and his wife Laura had taught their children the facts about their sexuality as they had grown up, telling them more as they were ready and able to understand. They tried hard to give their children the correct information as Paul and Laura realised that their culture taught lots of myths about sexuality that weren't very helpful or factual.

Model a healthy attitude towards your own sexuality

Paul and Laura also modelled a healthy approach to their own sexuality, one of mutual caring and love, and putting the other person's needs before their own. They talked about sex in a positive way, as a special gift for married couples.

Help your teens feel loved

Paul and Laura also helped their teens to feel loved, accepted and secure, because they knew that this would be a strong defence against the pressure to have sex at an early age. Teens who have their needs for love and acceptance met by their families are less likely to look for love and acceptance from others, and so they are less vulnerable to the temptation to have sex before marriage.

Help your teens to develop positive skills

They also found things that their teens were good at, and helped them to develop those interests. Tommy was musical, so they helped him to learn how to play an instrument and encouraged him to practise. He joined a music group and played regularly. Music gave him positive social and creative opportunities. Lyndon was good at sport and he was encouraged to join a team and go to practices and competitions. Melissa was quieter and liked to make beautiful things. She worked hard to make lovely pots and to sew unusual clothes, which she was able to sell, and start her own business. All these activities channelled their teen's energies

into positive actions. The teens felt good about their achievements, and they didn't need to find acceptance from their peers.

Help them feel good about themselves

Paul and Laura helped their teens to feel good about themselves. They weren't all beautiful and handsome, but the parents helped them to make the best of their looks by choosing flattering clothes, and finding attractive hairstyles. They made sure that their teens could feel confident about their appearance, so that they didn't need to find a sexual partner in order for them to feel attractive.

Involve them in constructive activities

Because the teens were involved in constructive activities and had parents who loved them and helped them to make the best of themselves, they were able to have self-confidence and self-respect. These two qualities help to protect a teen from being pressured by their friends into having sex. They are more able to stand up for what they believe and what they want, and less likely to do what everyone else is doing.

Encourage them to respect others

Being able to respect others is an important quality, too. Their sons needed to respect the girls around them, by being polite and careful with them. Paul taught his sons to treat women well, and to consider *their* needs, not just their own. He knew that when they were married they would be better husbands if they took the time to meet the needs of their wives. A wife who feels loved and cared for, and knows that her husband puts her needs ahead of his own, is much more likely to feel happy about her sexuality. Melissa needed to show her respect for the men around her by dressing and acting in ways that were modest, and not by provoking them sexually.

Encourage positive friendships

A healthy circle of positive friendships also provides a good support system for young people who are choosing to wait until they're married to have sex. When friends do activities in a group, all have similar goals and are encouraged to find fun things to do together, there is less of a need for close couple relationships to be formed.

Role play what to say when feeling pressured to have sex

Help your teens to develop some responses when others pressure them to become sexually involved. What can they say and do to protect themselves? Think up some responses together and practise them until they become easy to say.

Develop a sense of responsibility

Ever since the children were small Laura and Paul had encouraged their teens to be responsible for their own actions, big and small. Their teens knew that they had to be responsible for both themselves and their friends in the choices they would make about their relationships and their sexuality.

Talk about AIDS

Laura had a friend who was dying from AIDS. She spoke to the children openly about her experiences and her regrets. The children had direct experience of the illness when they went to visit her, and they could see for themselves the effect of making a wrong choice. It was even sadder for them to see her children, who also had HIV. They knew that one day their mother might die, and the children would be left all alone, and maybe they would be sick and die too. It felt so unfair to see them suffer for a mistake their parents had made.

Talk about pregnancy

Paul's sister had become pregnant at a very young age. The father of her baby had been an older, married man, who couldn't marry her. Finally, after many years, she did find a husband, but it had been a difficult life, with embarrassments, struggles and heartaches. It was good for the teens to hear her story too, and listen to the pain she had experienced because of the choices she had made. She had so many regrets. If she could have lived her life over again, she would not have made the same choice.

Discuss the consequences of wrong choices

Paul and Laura used the experience of their friends to open up a discussion of what happens when a wrong choice is made. They talked with their children about the options they might have if they made a mistake. What might they do if they realised that they were in a situation that could easily lead to sex? What could they do if they experienced powerful sexual feelings towards a member of the opposite sex before marriage? What would they do if they had sex before they were married? What choices would they have if their actions resulted in a pregnancy, or in a disease? What are some of the reasons why it's good to wait until marriage to have their first sexual experience? What would be some of the good things they would experience as a result of this choice?

Stay committed to your children

Paul and Laura let their children know that they would always be there for them. They taught them the right ways, but they also knew that young people could make mistakes at times. They wanted their children to know that whatever happened, whether they

waited to be married before having sex, or whether they didn't, their parents would always love them and forgive them, supporting them even if there was a baby, and even if they got ill with AIDS. They knew that their children would need that kind of security to help them through their teen years.

Accept and forgive them when they make mistakes

Even though they had made some good decisions as parents, and were doing the best they could to protect their children, Paul and Laura also knew that the children would have to choose for themselves. At least they knew that they had given them much more support, help and information than they had received as young people. If their teens made mistakes, they knew that they would forgive them. There would be no criticism, just tears, there would be no rejection, just acceptance.

Help your children to live without regrets

One thing that Laura and Paul were sure of was that no one ever regretted keeping sex for marriage, but nearly everyone regrets having sex before marriage. Help your children live without regrets. Help them stand up to sexual pressure and make good choices that last a lifetime, even into the next generation

Help with drugs and alcohol

The guidelines for helping your teen cope with sexual pressure can also be applied to supporting them in managing the pressure to try drugs and alcohol.

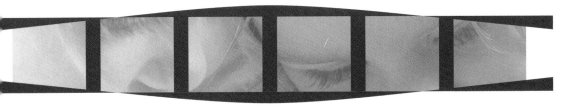

Chapter 3

Helping your family to grow spiritually

Building your children up with God's love

The most important gift we can give our children is the desire to love God and to follow and serve him.

Parents can help their children to become spiritually strong by setting positive examples. The children are encouraged by their parents' faith. Here are some ways that parents can help to build spiritually strong children.

Building spiritually strong children
- Have a strong relationship with God yourself, taking time to nurture your own spiritual growth through Bible study and reading.
- Talk to your children about your faith and your relationship with God.
- Talk about how God has been there for you through the difficult times. Talk about the doubts you used to have, and how your faith has been strengthened.
- Have an active prayer life and share your prayer experiences with your children. Pray for your children and with your children.

- Help your children to look for answers to prayer, but also to understand that God knows best, and sometimes the answers come in ways that we're not expecting, or even wanting.
- Have regular and interesting family worship times.
- Be positive as you talk about your church and its leaders. Be realistic, and help your children to understand that even church leaders may make mistakes, and encourage them to be supportive rather than critical.
- Have a practical understanding of God's grace. Grace is about God loving us no matter what we've done, but just because we're his children. This is one of the most beautiful aspects of the Christian faith.

- Collect stories of grace and share them with your children. One of the best messages you can give your children about God is that he is always there to love them and welcome them, no matter what they have done, just like in the story of the father and the prodigal son in Luke.
- Learn how to put grace into action in your family, offering forgiveness and acceptance when your children have made mistakes.
- Deal with your children the way God has patiently dealt with you.
- When you need to discipline your child, think first about the way God has disciplined you. Think about his tremendous love for you and for your child, and deal with your child gracefully rather than harshly. This is a powerful illustration of God's love. A child who lives with harsh discipline may grow to think that God is harsh, and will fear or reject him.
- Above all, love your children as God loves them, following 1 Corinthians 13 as a guide to practical parental love.

> 'Love the Lord your God with all your heart and with all your soul and with all your strength. These commandments that I give you today are to be upon your hearts. Impress them on your children. Talk about them when you sit at home and when you walk along the road, when you lie down and when you get up.'
> Deuteronomy 6:5-7.

Guidelines for great family worships

Here are some guidelines to help your family have special worships, and ideas to help you fill them with interesting activities for you and your children.

- As parents, make sure you are being filled spiritually through your own meaningful worship times.
- Keep the family worships simple. One idea is to use a devotional book suitable for the ages of your children, with short inspirational stories, during the week.
- Make weekend worship times as enjoyable as you can.
- Plan ahead for worships, and gather the materials you need well before time.
- Invest in the best spiritual material for your children! Buy good books from your local Christian Book Shop; seek out and hire good Christian videos; buy interesting Bible games and activity books.
- Keep worship times free of discipline and criticism. Make them positive experiences which are fun, interesting, brief, happy and loving. That is what the children will remember the most.
- Use the worships to teach the children Bible stories, learn how to make moral choices, follow God's guidance, develop a prayer relationship with God, learn about God's creation, memorise scriptures, experience the joy of serving others in practical ways, learn worshipful songs, and enjoy being a Christian.
- Remember that your children learn in different ways, and make sure that your worships contain practical illustrations, crafts, memorable stories and physical activities.
- Use the everyday events that happen to you and your children to teach them about God. Opportunities for spiritual teaching are all around you once you start to look, and these are often the best ways to help your children learn about God.

Creative Family Worship Activities

Following are some ideas for Bible-based activities for you to enjoy. Don't forget to invite singles, and other families to join in your activities with you!

- Choose a favourite Bible text and make a paper collage, or fabric banner to illustrate the verse.
- Design a cover for one of the books of the Bible, as if it were a single book. Each of you could choose a different book from the Bible. All kinds of art media could be used to design the covers.
- Design a poster encouraging people to pray.
- Put together a box of scraps of all kinds. Set a time limit for each person to create something beautiful or useful out of anything they can find in the box. Talk about the creation story, and how God can make something beautiful and useful out of very little. God also wants to make something beautiful out of our lives.
- Design badges to show how you feel about Jesus.
- Use modelling clay, or salt dough (2 parts plain white flour, 1 part salt, and water to mix to a mouldable consistency). Let each person model an object from the Bible. When the models are all finished, everyone has to try and guess what the object is, and from which Bible story it comes.
- If you have little rubber stamps or stickers, then try this activity. Give everyone a few plain index cards. Look at the pictures on the rubber stamps and try to find encouraging Bible texts that fit the theme of the stamp or sticker motif. Write out the text, and decorate it with the stickers or stamps. Keep the decorated texts in a pretty box. Add to them regularly to make your own promise box.
- Give everybody a plain sheet of paper to tear and fold into an object from the Bible for the others to guess. Alternatively, let each person take the name of another person in the group and create an imaginary, encouraging gift for the person out of the piece of paper. For example, the paper could be folded into a plane ticket for a trip abroad, a certificate, a car, a bed, a wallet full of paper money, etc!
- Choose a Bible story and then use toy building-bricks to create a Bible scene. What about the Tower of Babel? The Battle of Jericho? The Nativity? The New Jerusalem?

- Create Bible bookmarks of your favourite texts by cutting coloured cardboard into strips, and provide all kinds of art materials and paper scraps to decorate them. Make enough to share with friends, send with a letter, or include with a gift to someone.
- Let each person choose a simple story from the Bible and write it as a Rebus story. A Rebus story is a story where some of the words have been replaced by simple pictures. Collect all the stories together to give to a young child.
- Decorate sheets of blank white stickers with texts, encouraging words, and little pictures. Stick them onto envelopes as witness stickers.
- Create a 3D Bible scene in an empty box. Use pictures cut from old Christmas cards to make people, houses and backgrounds, adding other odds and ends to build up a little scene.
- Provide a selection of soft sweets, or, for a much healthier version, pieces of fruit and vegetables! Let each person make a model of themselves out of the bits and pieces, using cocktail sticks to connect the pieces together. Alternatively, make faces out of the food by arranging the pieces on paper plates. Talk about how God has made us all different, and why. Then eat your creations!

- Choose a parable from the Bible and illustrate it in comic strip form.
- Find a cassette or CD of a favourite Christian song. Create actions to illustrate the song. Practise the song well, and then put on a performance.
- Design the *inside* of Noah's Ark. What do you think it could have looked like? There needs to be a place for all the different animals, and all their food, and also a place for the humans, and their food.

Do all you can to make your worship time activities really imaginative!

Instant Bible games

It's helpful to have some simple Bible games that you can play together as a family. Here are some games that need only Bibles, pens and paper, and a few other simple items.

- Give everyone a Bible. Choose a chapter in the Bible and make sure everyone has found the chapter before you start. One person then begins to read aloud one of the verses in the chapter. The others see who can find the verse first and finish reading it aloud with the reader. The first person to begin reading it along with the reader wins the point. Take it in turns to choose chapters and to be the reader.
- Go through the alphabet naming as many Bible names as you can, beginning with each of the letters.
- Using modelling clay, toy bricks, or even pencil and paper, one person begins to shape or draw something from the Bible. The others try to be the first person to guess what is being made or drawn.
- Sit in a circle and start by one person saying the name of someone in the Bible. The next person has to say the name of someone in the Bible that starts with the last letter of the previous name, and so on. 'RutH' – 'HamaN' – 'NoaH' – 'HeroD', etc. No names can be repeated during the game.
- Each person thinks of

a Bible character and acts out clues to help the others guess who the character is. The person acting is not allowed to make any sounds or say any words, so all the clues have to be mimed.
- Write the letters A-Z down the side of a piece of paper. Find a Bible text beginning with each of the letters of the alphabet.
- Each person chooses a proverb from the book of Proverbs. They then have five minutes to draw a cartoon, or make up a drama sketch or mime (drama without words, only actions) about the proverb. The others have to try to guess which proverb has been chosen. To make it easier, each person can say which chapter his or her proverb is from.
- Give each person a carrier bag. They are then given five minutes to find as many things as they can that remind them of a Bible story. After five minutes everyone returns to show what has been found and the others have to guess which Bible story matches each object.
- Make acrostic sentences about Bible characters. An acrostic is where a Bible name is chosen, and then each of the letters in the name is the first letter of another word. For example, Jesus as an acrostic sentence could be:
JESUS - Joyfully Ever Saving Underachieving Souls

Memory verses — learning for life!

Helping your children to learn scripture verses plants the seeds of God's Word into their minds forever.

Make learning a Bible verse easy and enjoyable!

- Write a Bible verse on a rectangle of stiff card. Colour the card with designs that match the verse. Cut the card up into a jigsaw and then let your child put it back together again.
- Buy some alphabet pasta shapes (try a continental food shop) and put the shapes into a bowl on the table. Write a Bible verse clearly on a piece of paper. Work together to find the right letter shapes, and arrange them to spell out the whole verse. Some pasta shapes do not have all the letters in the English language, so be ready to substitute other letters. If you can't find alphabet pasta shapes, write the letters onto small squares of card, or use the letters from a purchased word game.
- Make secret code texts by writing out the first letter of each word in the text onto a small card. Give each child a card, after they have become familiar with the text. They can carry their card in their pocket and use the initial letters as a prompt to help them remember the whole text. For example: 'For God so loved the world' would be written 'FGSLTW'.
- Draw around your feet and cut out lots of cloth or paper feet shapes. Write the words of the verse to be learned on separate feet. Then let your children step from one paper foot to the next, reading the words for the text as they go. As they begin to learn the words, turn some of the feet over so the word no longer shows. Do this until all the feet are turned over and the verse has been learned.
- Let the children make up actions for a Bible verse to suit the words and act out the verse.
- Set the words of the verse to a well-known tune and make it into a song. Some Bible verses are already songs, and you could learn these with your family.
- Use the words of the Bible verse to create a word search or crossword puzzle for your children to do.
- Write out the verse using simple pictures in place of some of the words. Younger children who can't read can use the picture clues to help them learn the verse.
- Stand in a circle and throw a ball from one person to another across the middle of the circle, so no one quite knows who will catch the ball next. When the ball is caught, the catcher has to say the next word in the verse, before throwing the ball quickly to the next person. Stand further apart for a bigger challenge.
- Write the memory verse on a piece of paper and stick it where everyone will see it often, such as on a mirror or door.
- Make the Bible verse into an attractive poster. Or illustrate some of the Proverbs with cartoons.

Proverbs 17:14

Praying for your family

God wants to help our family relationships
and he loves it when we turn to him in prayer
for help with the most important
relationships in our lives.

Praying for your marriage

- If you're not used to praying
  for each other here are a
  few tips:
- Talk together for a few
  minutes about the
  concerns you each
  have for the day or
  week ahead. Then hold
  hands as you silently
  ask God to help your
  partner with the difficulties
  he or she will face. Squeeze
  each other's hands when
  you're finished.
- Even if your partner doesn't want to pray,
  you can pray for your marriage.
- Ask God to take control of your marriage
  and help you to make it the best it can be.
- Thank God for every positive thing in your
  relationship.
- Pray that God will help you in the areas
  that you find difficult.
- Pray for the qualities you need to be a
  better spouse, rather than focusing on
  changing your spouse.
- Ask God to forgive you for the mistakes
  you've made in your relationship, you may
  find it easier to apologise to your spouse.

Praying for your children

Here are some things you can pray for your
children:

- that God will take control of their lives, and
  be their Lord and King;

- that
  they'll
  discover
  what it
  means to
  be friends
  with
  God

- for their safety from
  danger, drugs, AIDS and negative
  influences;
- for their health;
- for their ability to make the right choices;
- for their understanding of right and wrong;
- for them to be able to respect others;
- for their choice of friends and activities;
- for their school and their teachers;
- for their future relationships and family life;
- that they'll know peace of mind, whatever
  they experience in life.

Teaching your children how to pray

- Write prayers on balloons and hang them
  from the ceiling.

- Encourage children to talk to God as they'd talk to a friend, telling him about their day, the things that made them happy, or sad, the things they're worried about, the things they want to say sorry and thank you for.
- Write little letters to God in a notebook. Write down the ways God answered the prayers for you and your children.
- Learn some traditional prayers from a children's book of prayers, or learn The Lord's Prayer. Many children still pray this in school.
- Make a little booklet of things to thank God for and let your children cut out pictures to stick in the book.
- Write prayers about sick people on small strips of paper. Roll them up and keep them in a large jar,

Prayer is talking to God like a friend.

'Don't fret or worry. Instead of worrying, pray.
Let petitions and praises shape your worries into prayers, letting God know your concerns. Before you know it, a sense of God's wholeness, everything coming together for good, will come and settle down. It's wonderful what happens when Christ displaces worry at the centre of your life.'
Philippians 4:6,7, The Message.

Remember that God hears all our prayers. He answers some, 'Yes,' some 'No,' some 'Wait,' and some 'I've got an even better idea!'

like a bottle of tablets. Every now and then tip out the paper 'tablets' and see who's better now. Stick a star on those prayers to remind you that God hears prayers for healing.
- Write a favourite prayer using a computer graphic programme, pre-printed stationery, or your own artwork, to illustrate it. Frame it as a picture for your child's room.
- Find some contemporary children's prayer books for prayers that deal with children's everyday experiences. When you don't know what to say, choose a prayer from the book to help you get started.
- It's really comforting to let your children know they can talk to God anytime and anywhere, and that God can help them when they're frightened, or when they don't know what to do.

Creative prayer ideas for families

Try praying in a new way with your family. Prayer doesn't have to be kneeling down with our hands together and eyes closed. Just as God communicates with us in lots of different ways, so he is happy for us to communicate with him in different ways too. He is delighted when our children are excited about praying to him.

- Make a small bag filled with objects that can help remind your children about things to pray for. At prayer time let each person choose one or more objects from the bag, and use these items to guide their prayers. For example, include photos of people to pray for, plastic food as reminders to thank God for providing their food, a toy car to remind them to pray for safekeeping as they travel, etc.
- Go through the alphabet together finding aspects of God to praise! Either take it in turns to find one aspect per letter, or brainstorm as a group, exploring each letter until you can think of no more words!

> I praise you, God, because you are
> Amazing, Adorable, Authentic, Always there . . .
> I praise you, God, because you are
> Beautiful, Bountiful, Blessed . . .
> Creative, Comforting . . . Delivering, etc.

- Try a teaspoon prayer. The cooking term for a teaspoon is TSP, and these letters stand for Thank You, Sorry and Please.

Pass a teaspoon around the group and each say 'Thank you, God, for . . .', then 'I'm sorry, God, that I . . .', then 'Please, God . . .'

- Wrap a box in attractive paper and decorate it like a big present. Using large white stickers, let everyone write thank-you notes to God for the gifts he has given them. Then let everyone come forward and stick his or her thank-you note onto the gift. Read all the notes out as a prayer.
- Find beautiful pictures of nature scenes. Old calendars are useful. Looking at the pictures write down the things in the pictures that remind you of God's love, power, creativity, gentleness, etc. Collect the phrases and statements together and arrange them into a psalm of praise.

As you walk along the way...

Walking in nature creates wonderful opportunities to teach children about God's creation. Here are some ideas to help you make the most of walking with your children:

Have a scavenger hunt. Make a list of twenty things to be found on a nature walk, copy the list for each person, and give each one a medium sized bag in which to collect their finds! Some ideas for the list are:

A feather
A piece of egg-shell
Something perfectly smooth
Something that reminds you of an Old Testament story
Something that reminds you of a parable
Something which reminds you of God's love
Something blue
Some animal hair or fluff
A pretty stone
Three different kinds of grass

Avoid including items that could endanger the children or the environment and make sure the area is safe. Perhaps they could wear some disposable gloves to protect their hands.

- Give each child a small piece of card with a strip of double-sided sticky tape on one side of the card. Ask the children to see how many different colours they can find in the world around them. Show them that there are many shades of green in nature, and yellow, brown, etc. **Remind them to take only tiny pieces of petals, so that whole flowers are not destroyed.** See if they can fill their card with lots of different colours. Thank God for all the variety and beauty he has created.
- Try a parable walk. As you walk look for different things that tell parables about God's love and care for us. For example, in Britain there are plants called nettles that can cause nasty itchy spots if the leaves touch human skin. Close to nettle there are usually some dock leaves growing. When a dock leaf is rubbed over the nettle spots, the pain is relieved. The nettles can be a parable of our sin and the dock leaves can remind us of God's love and healing forgiveness.
- As you walk, write down objects that remind you of Bible stories. Find a clearing in which to sit and read your notes on the objects seen, getting the others to guess the Bible story with which the object is connected.
- Choose a Bible story, proverb or parable and, without letting others know which story it is, gather simple things along the pathway that you can use to make an arrangement to illustrate the story. At the end of the walk, each of you can spend a few minutes creating your arrangement or scene, and then the others can try to guess which story is being illustrated.

Children can witness too!

Where it is safe to do so, you can encourage your children to witness to their friends in simple ways.

One of the best ways that they can witness is by being a caring friend to those they know, showing love and unselfishness, and standing up for what is right, even when it's difficult. This can be hard to do, and they will need your encouragement. But there are other things children can do to help others learn more about Jesus.

- Children often love to help distribute outreach cards. Teach them how to be good witnesses by walking only on pathways, and being courteous. Always have an adult close by to keep the children safe.
- Encourage children to pray regularly for the conversion of a few people they know.
- Have a themed party for your child's birthday, such as Noah's Ark, and show a Bible Story video at the party, and give tiny books about Noah in the party bags, with plastic animals, rainbow stickers, etc.
- Invite all their friends to Holiday Bible School.
- When a new baby is born, look in Christian bookshops for a gift book for the parents that has some spiritual content too.
- Develop a really lively and interesting family worship together, and then let your children invite a friend for supper, and to share in the worship time. Light some candles and create a cosy atmosphere.
- If your children are in a special event at church, invite non-Christian relatives along to share the occasion.
- Buy or design and make a witnessing t-shirt for your children to wear. Make sure it is tasteful and attractive.
- Involve the church children in a community outreach project, or aid project, and invite the local paper to write a report about them.
- Children can have pen pals, and email friends, with whom they can share their faith in a non-threatening way.
- Do all you can to make sure that your children are delighting in their Christianity, and that their experience of God is fresh, exciting and enjoyable. They will be naturally exuberant about their faith, and that is an incredible witness to others.

Top Twenty ways you can serve others as a family

Helping to develop a positive attitude towards serving others is an important part of raising children. Acts of service encourage children to be unselfish, and to find delight in thinking about ways to help others. One of the best ways to teach children about service is to involve them in the various methods you employ to help others.

1 Volunteer to take a programme together at your church. Team up with another family, or singles you know well, and put on a programme for the families of your church.

2 Volunteer, as a family, to take part in the church service one week. You could write out a prayer together, and take turns to read different sections of the prayer. You could do a musical item, tell and illustrate the children's story, announce the hymns, or take up the offering.

3 Offer to do a clean-up project at your church. Tidy up the grounds, pull out the weeds, paint the toilets, decorate the children's rooms, offer to run a childcare service once a quarter, arrange the flowers together, etc.

4 Adopt an elderly person with no grandchildren close by as an extra grandparent. Invite the grandparent to your home, do jobs for him or her around the house and garden. Take the grandparent with you on special outings. Find little cards and gifts to brighten his or her life. Find out their needs, likes and dislikes, and ways you can be of most help.

5 Create a secret helping project! Find someone in real need and surprise the person by meeting their needs secretly and unexpectedly! Offer to mow lawns for busy people. Bake delicious food for a single-parent family, and leave it on their doorstep. Weed gardens for people who are getting too old to manage. Leave parcels on their doorstep, such as food, clothes and toys, etc. Be sure everything is clean and good quality. Children enjoy the fun of being part of a secret surprise, and this can help to encourage them to be a part of a project.

6 If you have older children, volunteer for a mission service project instead of a holiday, and give your children a taste of mission service. Make sure that you are well prepared for the trip.

7 Start a family ministry. Have a family counsel and brainstorm some ideas of all the ways your family could serve others in your community. Choose one of the projects, and plan how your family can minister effectively. You could be part of a

soup-run team, and everyone could help to make the soup, and take it onto the streets to feed the homeless people. Maybe you could explore your talents and use them in different ways, such as a puppet ministry telling Bible stories to children, a ministry to retirement homes, a befriending ministry, or a hospitality ministry.

8 Help young children to serve others. Teach them by practice and role play how to treat guests in your home, how to welcome people at the front door, show them where to put their coats, and where the bathroom is, etc. The child can also ask guests if they would like a drink, and learn how to pour water or juice into pretty glasses, not too full, and carry them to the guests.

9 Whenever possible, when you are involved in some type of service yourself, think of ways to involve the children, so they will come to see serving others as an important, loving and happy thing to do.

10 Encourage children to save money in a little box throughout the year, to help with a special project, or to choose and buy a toy for a needy child.

11 Borrow promotional videos or read literature from several mission or charitable organisations to show to your children, to expand their understanding of the world, and the many different needs people have.

12 If you can afford to do so, sponsor a child at a mission school. Choose a reputable organisation that offers regular information about the child, and be willing to follow their guidelines about gift giving and letter writing. It is good for children to see a long-term, service-project unfold, and to be involved in the life of a child

who has a very different lifestyle.

13 Encourage your children to come up with their own ideas for service, and be willing to help them follow through with the ideas that they have.

14 Expose your older children to a variety of people groups that they may not normally encounter. Visit a shelter for teenage mothers, a prison, a drug rehabilitation centre, a home for people with learning difficulties, a day centre for blind people, etc. Visits like these will heighten your child's awareness of the needs of others. Encourage the children to write down thoughtful and considerate questions that they would like to ask the people they visit in these centres, so that they can learn the most they can from the experience. Visit the place yourself, beforehand, and check out any rules for visitors, and what the child can expect to experience by making the visit.

15 When you are having visitors in your home, plan the event with the whole family, and give everyone a special part to play. One child can choose the music, and operate the stereo, or play their instrument; another can set the table, or help with making a flower arrangement, or serving drinks. The children can also help to choose the menu for the meal, help to make the food, and plan after-meal activities. The children can decorate pretty cards and write Bible promises on the cards to tuck into the napkins. The cards can be read while waiting for the dessert to be served, and each person could make a comment about the text on their card.

16 Try to teach your children helping skills. Teach them sewing skills, how to mend clothes, sew on buttons, care for small children, etc. Another time teach the children how to use a screwdriver, change a tyre, fix things properly, do first aid, and decorate interior walls without making a (big) mess. Take them into the garden and teach them the difference between weeds and flowers, or seedling vegetables. Not only are these skills necessary for life, but they will also increase the child's confidence and potential for service.

17 Make a game in your family of doing secret things to help others. Once a week, let each person in the family tell what they have done to help their teacher, school-friends, siblings, parents, and even complete strangers. This encourages the children to think about serving others, and using their own initiative to do so.

18 Encourage your children to join in community service projects that are sometimes advertised locally. If your church has a community services department, find out if there is anything your family could usefully do to help them, too.

19 Enrol for classes that will help develop service skills, such as junior first aid classes, baby-sitters' training courses, youth award schemes, and environmental training schemes, etc.

20 Above all, show your children that service is fun! Show them the joy there is in helping others, rather than focusing on self! Teach them that when we serve others, it is as though we are serving Jesus himself!

Characteristics to nurture in your children
Read Galatians 5:22-23

Love • by discovering an all-loving God, experiencing love in action within the family, and loving others the way God wants them to experience his love.

Joy • looking for the ways God is showing his love and beauty, even in the most difficult of situations.

Peace • being content and unselfish, being happy with others when they have something to be happy about, rather than being jealous.

Patience • being willing to wait for things to happen in God's time.

Kindness • doing helpful and loving things for others, thinking about what others need rather than about what they themselves want.

Goodness • choosing to behave lovingly towards others.

Faithfulness • having faith in God, and also doing the small things in life with consistency and dedication as well as the bigger things.

Gentleness • being careful of those who are younger, weaker or more vulnerable.

Self-control • learning to wait until last and letting others go first.

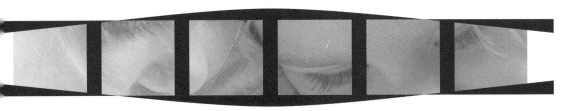

Chapter 4

Building a strong marriage

Preparing for marriage

The decision to marry someone is one of the most important decisions we ever make.

When it's time to consider marriage, pray, pray and pray again. You need all the wisdom and discernment God can give you.

In some cultures it is usual for the family to arrange the marriage, but in other cultures the couple decide to marry each other. In either case, it can be useful for the couple to spend some time thinking and praying carefully about what marriage will mean for them both.

Here are some ideas to help you prepare well for your marriage:
- Know each other for at least a year so that you have seen each other in different seasons and circumstances.
- Look at how your future husband or wife relates to their opposite sex parent. A husband-to-be who treats his mother disrespectfully is likely to treat his wife in a similar manner.
- Ask others you trust what they think about your planned marriage and consider their counsel carefully.
- If you feel you are being pressured into marriage, step back from the relationship and take a break for a month to examine your thoughts. The need to leave home, being pregnant, or having been sexually involved with each other do not form a good basis for a happy and secure marriage.
- Explore together how you think about important issues such as money, child discipline, faith, relations, and roles, etc. Be honest with each

other, and when you disagree, take the time to listen to each other, and understand each other's perspective. Then negotiate a happy solution for you both. If there is something you discover about the

> **'For this reason a man will leave his father and mother, and be united to his wife, and the two will become one flesh. So they are no longer two, but one. Therefore what God has joined together, let man not separate.'**
> Matthew 19:5, 6.

other person that you think would be difficult to live with, don't be afraid to end the relationship before you are married.

- If you are from different cultures, explore each of your cultures very carefully and decide how you might blend the two together. You need to be able to meet each other in a place of your own creating between the two cultures, but this is never an easy task.
- Be very cautious if anything about the other person disturbs you. Perhaps you have seen them become very angry, or violent, or perhaps they are silent and moody from time to time, or speak and behave irrationally for your culture. Perhaps you are concerned about their use of drugs or alcohol. Don't overlook such things; ask about them, and consider whether it would be wise for you to spend the rest of your life with this person.
- Think carefully together about your future living arrangements. The Scriptures recommend leaving our parents' homes, joining together, and then becoming one flesh.
- Ask yourselves the following

questions and take plenty of time to answer them honestly and thoroughly:

- What role will God and our faith have in our new family?
- How will we make God the Lord of our home?
- Where will we live?
- Who will work, and where?
- How long will we wait before having children?
- What choices do we feel happy exploring if we find that we can't have children of our own?
- How will we manage our money?
- How will we manage marriage as the equal partnership

> **It's better to break an engagement than it is to break a marriage.**

designed by God in the Garden of Eden?
- How much involvement in *our* family will we expect from our different families of origin?
- How will we manage any disagreements?
- How does my spouse-to-be handle disappointments? Does he or she forgive easily?
- How will we make time to work on our marriage so it's the best it can be?
- What family traditions would we each like to bring into our new home?
- What family patterns across the generations would we like to change in our family?
  - Make a list of the usual tasks of a home and talk about who will take responsibility for the different tasks. Look at who has different skills, rather than sharing out the tasks according to gender or traditional roles.

Healthy marriages are based on commitment for life to God and to each other, and on learning every day how to help the other person feel loved and special.

Cohabitation – living together before marriage

More and more couples are trying to prepare for marriage by living together to see if they are suited to each other. They feel that they are doing the best thing for their relationship by testing it out before committing themselves. But recent research into these relationships shows that is not the best kind of pre-marital experiment.

> **Sex before marriage usually leads to regrets. No one ever regretted waiting until marriage to have sex.**

Here are some of the facts about cohabitation:
- Couples who live together for a time before marriage are much more likely to split up later.
- Good marriages are based on commitment. Living together without being married shows a lack of commitment right from the start, because the relationship can be ended at any time.
- Whenever a couple become sexually involved, the sexual side is often more important than getting to know each other better, and making good decisions.
- Women are especially vulnerable in a cohabiting relationship. They are more likely to suffer from anxiety, have unwelcome pregnancies, and be victims of domestic violence.

- Men are more likely to be unfaithful. One quarter of cohabiting men are unfaithful to their partners.
- Both partners are more likely to be unhealthy, have addictions, have less money and live shorter lives than married couples.
- When a cohabiting couple break up it can be just as painful and difficult as a divorce.
- Married couples are more likely to look for solutions to any difficulties in their relationships.
- When children are born to a cohabiting couple the greatest fear, as they grow older, is that their home will break up.
- First-time cohabiting couples are five times more likely to break up than a first-time married couple.
- Children in a secure married family are more likely to do well at school, be healthier, and be more successful in their work when they are adults. They are also much more likely to have good marriages of their own.

Give your marriage the best possible chance by choosing to wait until you are married before living together and starting a sexual relationship.

Creating a wedding on a budget

With some weddings costing several thousand pounds, many couples are choosing to live together for a while in order to save money for their big day. As cohabitation can have a negative effect on a subsequent marriage, maybe some ideas about creating a beautiful wedding for less money could be helpful for young couples thinking about marriage.

Ideas for themes
- Explore wedding traditions from other cultures and choose one or two new ideas to make your wedding extra special.
- Look for simple and creative ways to make the wedding memorable rather than expensive and elaborate ways.

Rings
- Use the German tradition of wearing the wedding ring on the ring finger of the opposite hand during the engagement.
- Buy second-hand rings or use ones handed down through the family.
- Buy a simple ring and have a special message engraved inside to personalise it.

Invitations
- These can be created attractively and simply using a computer. To add interest, print onto tracing paper, in grey to

look like silver, or in another colour, punch holes and tie onto folded card using narrow, coloured ribbons.
- Friends skilled in crafts could help to rubberstamp and emboss designs on invitations, or use calligraphy skills that can be photocopied.
- Look at all kinds of hand-made cards to find ideas to use in your designs at a fraction of the cost.
- The designs can be adapted and used for the programme, the place cards and menu, etc, if needed.

Clothes
- Borrow from others.
- Buy second-hand and sell on again for the same price.
- Buy from a charity shop and donate back.
- Explore ethnic wedding clothing choices that support projects in developing countries.
- Buy clothes that can be worn again later.
- Sew wedding clothes for a fraction of the cost, using simple fabrics like cotton and muslin rather than silks and satins.

Flowers
- Use the church's flowers from the weekend services, working with the flower arranger on the choice of colours.
- Choose simple flowers and carry a small bunch of lilies or daisies with some trailing ivy.
- Use silk flower posies that can be reused at other weddings.
- Use small trees, such as evergreens or bay trees, that can be decorated with co-

ordinating ribbons and used outside and inside the church, and at the reception, and then be planted in the couple's garden (perhaps these could be a wedding gift from a friend).
- Fresh flowers could be given to a nursing home, or housebound person after the service.

Music
- Friends who are musical could play at the service and the reception.
- Use CD player for background music.

Photos
- Ask a friend to take the photos, especially with a digital camera that can be used together with a computer to create special effects.
- Tape record the words of the service instead of having a video.
- Use home-video rather than a professional photographer.

- Ask people to look out for unusual shots to photograph to add a fresh dimension to the album. Perhaps you could run a competition for the guests, offering a prize for the best wedding photo submitted within a month of the wedding.
- Ask someone with a video camera to interview guests about their best memories of the couple, or their favourite relationship tips, etc to give to the couple or even play during the reception.

Transport
- Borrow, or use the car of a friend or family member.
- Choose an unusual form of transport, or even a taxi.
- Walk to the church, if it is local, with a parade of friends all holding tall colourful flowers, like gladioli. Friends can make an arch of flowers for the couple, or bride alone, to enter the church.

Hair
- Choose a simple style that you or a friend can do, and add fresh flowers for a special look.

Food
- Organise friends to bring donated dishes to provide a buffet.
- Buy food from a wholesale food outlet to make catering easy and cut costs.
- Serve just cake, drinks and nibbles.
- Serve an *agape* meal using fruits, nuts, breads and other simple foods.
- Invite friends to bring a bottle.
- Use glasses loaned from friends – make a small mark underneath with a waterproof pen to indicate whose glasses are whose so that they can be returned later.
- Use plain white sheets as tablecloths that can be given to the couple as a wedding present.
- Use ivy and wild flowers in abundance to provide simple and free table decorations.

Cake
- Purchase ready-made and iced cakes from a supermarket.
- Use one small, decorated cake, and cut up ready-made cakes for serving.
- Decorate cakes with curled ribbons, lace, or fresh flowers for a quick and simple stylish finish.
- Decorate cakes using simple shapes cut from rolled icing with a shaped cutter, such as hearts or ivy leaves.
- Explore the wedding cakes used by other cultures and see if something else appeals to you.

Wedding with a difference
- Do something at the wedding that will inspire and encourage other married couples.
- Encourage other couples to reaffirm vows.

- Pass around a blank book for guests to write in their best tips for a happy marriage, or ideas for special nights out.
- Create a special presentation on PowerPoint for the wedding service or reception to add something unique to the event – this could be emailed to friends who couldn't come.

Churches can help by

- Being eco-friendly by providing simple decorations that can be used at weddings.
- Providing stain resistant, easy-care white tablecloths that can be used for special occasions.
- Developing a loan service for many items needed for weddings to help couples cut the cost.
  - Working together as a community to create special weddings for couples attending the church.

Secrets of a successful marriage

Some of the best secrets of a successful marriage are found in 1 Corinthians 13.

Love is patient

- Love is happy to wait for the other person, and to give him all the time he needs. Love doesn't get frustrated, and love doesn't nag. Love waits for *God* to change the other person.
- How will I show more patience towards my spouse, by letting God deal with imperfections, while I show my unconditional and accepting love?

Love is kind

- Love thinks of new ways to be tender and affectionate towards the other person, and is mature enough to put their needs first.
- How will I show kindness to my spouse, by putting their needs before my own desires?

Love does not boast

- Love builds up the other person, rather than himself or herself. Love looks for ways to show the other person approval and honour, and to help him feel valued. Love boasts about the other person, and builds her up in front of friends, family, colleagues and children. Love encourages the other person to reach goals and do well.

- How will I build up my spouse, and help him or her to know their value in God's eyes and mine? How will I help my spouse towards his or her goals?

Love is not proud

- Love is humble and is willing to do any job, however small, dirty or menial, to help the loved one.
- What things will I do to support my spouse in his or her role? What things do I think are beneath me to do? Why do I think that and how can I change my attitude?

Love is not rude

- Love is polite and respectful, even in the everyday routines of life. Love tries not to do anything that causes offence to the loved one, or knowingly irritates or frustrates. Love is appreciative and grateful.
- How will I be courteous towards my spouse, and live so that I don't offend him or annoy her? How will I show my love and appreciation for my spouse?

Love is not self-seeking

- Love finds ways to meet the other person's needs, and doesn't demand that its own needs are met first.
  - How will I discover my spouse's emotional and practical needs, and do all I can to meet them?

Love is not easily angered

- Love takes a long time to become angry. It is slow to anger and quick to love. It believes the best things about other people, and looks for the good in what they say and do. Love deals with conflicts and differences in a gentle and mutual way.
- How will I handle the next conflict with my spouse in a gentle and calm manner? How will I show that I believe the best about my spouse?

Love keeps no record of wrongs

- Love is forgiving, and gracious, and doesn't hold grudges. Love also lives so that it doesn't take advantage of the forgiveness and grace of others.

- How will I show forgiveness and grace towards my spouse when he or she makes a mistake?

Love does not delight in evil but rejoices with the truth

- A loving couple want to discover God's plan for their relationship. They find delight in doing God's will and in learning more about his truth together.
- How will we discover God's will together? What steps will we take to grow in our understanding of his love for each of us?

Love always protects

- Love always helps the loved one to feel safe and secure from any threat within the relationship, or from any threat from outside of the relationship. This means that love protects the loved one from violence, and does everything to help him or her feel safe. Love stays committed to the relationship, and to making it better.
- How will I show my commitment to my spouse? How can I ensure that he or she always feels safe with me around?

Love always trusts

- Love trusts that the other person will live up to his trust. Love makes sure that it never abuses any trust, and that it remains faithful

to the marriage.
- How will I honour my spouse's trust in me?

Love always hopes

- Love has many hopes for the future. Love reframes today's disappointments into hopes for the future. Love always provides something for the other person to look forward to.
- What hopes do I have for our marriage? What will I do to make them a reality? What promise can I make to my spouse so that he or she will have something to look forward to each week or each month?

Love always perseveres

- Love keeps on loving, even when it isn't being loved in return, or when changes don't seem to happen very quickly.
- Where do I need to show more perseverance in my love towards my spouse?

Love never fails

- When in doubt, do the most loving thing you can for your spouse. Comfort them when they are sad, support them when they are overwhelmed, be happy with them when good things happen in their life.
- What is the most loving thing I could do for my spouse this week?

Solving problems peacefully

Even the happiest and closest marriages encounter challenges from time to time. When two different human beings live closely together, as in a marriage, there will naturally be times when there are disagreements or differing perspectives on a situation.

- Often the closer we become, the more likely it is that we will face conflicts between us.
- Conflicts are a healthy and normal part of a good relationship.
- The conflict is not the problem; it's how we handle the conflict that decides whether we will be pushed further apart, or brought closer together.
- When there are conflicting and differing opinions, it can be an opportunity to learn more about each other, and increase the closeness of the relationship.
- For this to happen, each person needs to be free to talk about how the situation makes her feel, and to know that the other person has taken the time to listen to her, without feeling that her ideas are inferior or superior to the other person's ideas.
- Sometimes it's important for us to spend time thinking about where our ideas about something have originated, and whether it's time to change those ideas.
- After each conflict, try to come together, forgive each other, and show love to one another, so that the conflict doesn't push you apart.
- Make it your goal to understand the other person, rather than to be understood yourself.

Problem Discussion

- Before you try to solve a problem or conflict it's important for everyone involved to be able to say how they feel about the situation, and to know that views expressed have been heard and understood.

This is the most important part of solving the problem.

- It is important to separate the *discussion* of a particular problem from the *solution* to a problem.
- First discuss the problem. Take it in turns to be the speaker or the listener. Give the speaker something to hold, like a spoon or a handkerchief.

> **'If it is possible, as far as it depends on you, live at peace with everyone.'**
> Romans 12:18.

- The speaker says how he or she feels about the situation, in a few short sentences at a time. The listener only describes what he or she has heard the speaker say, to check that they have understood the speaker correctly. This is to make sure that there are no misunderstandings that can lead to further problems.
- After the speaker feels that he or she has been heard and understood, the speaker and listener switch roles.
- Discuss the problem until both of you agree that you have had a good discussion of the issues involved, and when you both feel you have heard and understood the other person's feelings and points of view.
- Don't try to shorten the discussion phase by trying to solve the problem too quickly, such as by saying something like: 'I'll do whatever you say I should.'

'If one gives an answer before hearing, it is folly and shame.' Proverbs 18:13, NRSV.

Prayer

- Take time to be guided by the Holy Spirit in what you do.
- Pray silently or aloud, together or apart – the important thing is to acknowledge God's wisdom in the matter.
- Prayer can bring you together as a couple.

'Trust in the Lord with all your heart, and lean not on your own understanding; in all your ways acknowledge him, and he shall direct your paths.' Proverbs 3:5, NKJV

> **'Live in harmony with one another.'**
> Romans 12:16.

Working on the problem

- Choose one part of the problem to deal with at one time.
- Suggest any ideas that come to mind, no matter how wild, funny or apparently impractical. Funny ideas help to reduce tension!
- Write all the ideas down.
- Go through the list evaluating the ideas, and looking at different combinations of ideas.
- Choose a specific solution that would work well for both of you, considering each other's feelings and needs.

'Finally, all of you, live in harmony with one another; be sympathetic, love as brothers, be compassionate and humble.' 1 Peter 3:8.

Follow Up

- Agree to try the solution for a fixed period of time to see if it works.

- Evaluate the solution and see if it needs to be changed at all.
- If you get stuck anywhere, you may need to spend more time discussing the problem.

Remember

- Many problems can be solved when plenty of time is taken for open discussion, and each person has a sense of being understood.
- Some problems need specific, practical solutions.
- Some problems have no solution, but these are quite rare.
- Don't let any problem ruin your marriage, or any other relationship. Go back to the problem discussion stage if you need to.
- What may seem unsolvable now may find a solution later. Keep praying for God to show you what to do.

Why do I think and behave the way I do?

When you are feeling strongly about something, spend a few moments thinking why you feel, behave, and think the way you do.

This can help you to decide where you may need to make some changes, or it may help you explain your thoughts and ideas to your spouse.

- My parents always said . . . or did . . .
- Other significant adults always said . . . or did . . .
- My friends and others the same age as me say . . . and do . . .
- I have had experiences in my life that have shaped the way I think, feel, and behave in relation to this topic and they were . . .
- My family told stories that relate to this idea, which help guide my thoughts and behaviours. Those stories are of . . .
- In this situation my greatest fear is . . .
- In this situation my greatest hope is . . .

Investing in your own marriage
by Cyril Sweeney*

Many affairs start because spouses stop investing in their own marriage relationship.

> **'Relish life with the spouse you love, each and every day of your precarious life.'**
> Ecclesiastes 9:9, The Message.

When their marriages seem dry and boring, or they feel unappreciated, they become vulnerable when other relationships offer something new and interesting, or someone else shows them a little appreciation.

But an extra-marital affair has many hidden costs, such as deceit, lack of trust, disease, pain, guilt, and the breakdown of relationships and the family. An affair is a high-risk investment. It's much safer to invest in the relationship you already have, and make that the special relationship you really want.

How to have an affair with your spouse!
- Encourage the spiritual growth of your marriage.
- Treat your spouse with sincere respect as a person of worth and value.
- Take notes of your spouse's work, dress, and achievements and compliment often.
- Be supportive of your spouse in times of failure, disappointments and sad moments.
- Build your spouse up with appreciative words.
  - Be prepared to share prime time with your spouse without feeling impatient.
  - Be open and honest in expressing your feelings to your partner.
  - Enjoy doing things together.
- Tell your spouse by words, deeds and actions that he or she is the number one human being in your life.
  - Encourage your partner to develop talents and abilities.
  - Show interest in your spouse's job and activities.

- Let your spouse know that you appreciate all the things they do to make your marriage happy.
- Be careful of your relationships with the opposite sex. Never give your spouse reason to be jealous or suspicious.
- Enjoy giving and receiving expressions of affection, touching, kissing, hugging etc.
- Make an effort to keep yourself attractive and appealing to your spouse.

The best person to share a love affair with is your own spouse.

- Take an active part in showing genuine pleasure and love in your sex life with your spouse.
- Accept your spouse 'as is' and do not attempt a remake by nagging, comparing or criticising.
- Think of special things to do for your spouse to make him or her happy.
- Forgive your spouse easily when she or he does something that hurts you.
- Feel totally satisfied with your spouse – be glad that you married to him or her!
- Always have a listening ear for your spouse when he or she wants to communicate.

Could I have an extra-marital affair?

Any marriage can be vulnerable to an affair.

Many people think it will never happen to them, and then an affair creeps slowly into their lives and takes them by surprise.

If you don't think it will ever happen to you, try asking yourself the following questions:

- **Do I work with people of the opposite sex?**
- **Do I travel to work with people of the opposite sex?**
- **Am I in any group, without my spouse, where I meet people of the opposite sex, such as a sports club, church choir, study class, etc?**
- **Do I have access to a telephone, a mobile phone, or the Internet?**
- **Do I ever look at people of the opposite sex?**
- **Do I ever step outside of my home?**

If you can answer yes to any of the above questions then you may be vulnerable!

Make sure you take the time to invest actively in your own marriage relationship.

* Cyril Sweeney is a minister with experience in counselling.

Being best friends with your spouse

Friendship takes time and planning. We need to plan good friendship time into the relationships we treasure, whether it's our marriage, our children, our parents, or our friends.

So often we have great times with our friends, but seem to forget that we can also have a wonderful friendship with our spouse!

Think of all the things you've done with your friends in the past few weeks and then think about how many of those things you've also done with your spouse.

Investing in your friendship together as a married couple can mean that your life is enriched, and your marriage is the happy relationship God designed it to be.

Friends and lovers
- Think about your marriage as a very special friendship, and do all you can to enjoy being together and to make the other person happy.
- Set aside a specific time for friendship activities, and do some of those things together that you've been doing with other friends, such as

chatting, taking a trip to town together, or sitting down and playing a game together.
- Keep the special friendship moments happy and peaceful, and protect them from being disturbed by arguments and conflicts.
- Enjoy listening to each other, and sharing your dreams for your marriage, and your future.
- Listen to each other as you would listen to a friend; share your concerns, the things you enjoy, and the things you appreciate about each other.
- Discover the special things your spouse likes you to do for him or her.

Married couples who make the time to have happy moments together, are healthier and happier.

The best way to have happy times in your relationship is to set a clear, regular time for yourselves to enjoy being together as a couple. Then fill that special time with lots of happy moments!

Creating special memories together

This is a simple way of having fun as a couple!

- Each take a sheet of paper and write down ten things you would really like to do with your spouse; things that you've always wanted to do; things that you haven't done for years; things that would be really fun, or even crazy!
- Give each other your lists.
- Each month one of you chooses one thing to do from the other's list, and takes the responsibility for planning a special time together.
- So, for the first month the husband chooses something from the wife's list.
- He tells her what he's chosen and then she writes down

> **'Rejoice in the wife of your youth.'**
> Proverbs 5:18.

> **'A cheerful heart is good medicine.'**
> Proverbs 17:22.

everything that would make the occasion really special for her, so that he knows just what to do, what food to buy, where to take her and which book to read.

- Maybe she would like to have a picnic meal in a grassy place next to a river, and read a book together. The husband can buy some delicious food, and pack it into a basket with a rug to sit on, napkins, drink, cups, sun-shade, a good book, and anything else that might be needed. He would arrange for a babysitter and take care of the transportation and everything else that would make the moment special.
- As you spend time doing what your spouse has chosen, be happy with her, and enter into the activity wholeheartedly, knowing that next time it will be your turn to choose the activity!
- It doesn't have to cost a lot of money to have special times together as a couple. Often the simplest pleasures are the most memorable because we have to take more time and effort to make them happen.

Doing special things for each other

- Take a sheet of paper and write at the top: 'I really love it when you . . .'
- Then list ten things that you love your spouse doing for you, such as bringing you flowers, cooking a favourite meal, giving you a back rub, or letting you have an extra stay in bed one morning by getting up with the children.
- Share your lists with each other and then try to do the things on the list whenever you can.

Laugh together!
- Read funny books about married life, or books of cartoons about marriage.
- Cut cartoons from newspapers that really fit the occasion.
- Choose each other funny greetings cards.
- Share funny stories about the things you've seen, heard and done during the day.
- Discover the special things about each other's sense of humour.
- Learn to laugh when things don't go according to plan, but protect your spouse from feeling that they are being ridiculed or made fun of.
- Watch a funny film or video together.
- Play a game that requires you to do funny things, or contains funny questions. Play to let the other person win!
- Do some of the fun things you used to do as children, such as building a sandcastle, playing ball together, flying a kite, or even dropping sticks into a river and racing them down stream to see whose goes the furthest (Pooh-sticks)!

Ideas for fun and simple dates
- Go for a walk in the evening in a lovely place and watch the sunset together.
- Go to a café and order a simple drink. Linger as long as you can and share the happy and funny memories you have about your marriage.
- Try a new activity that neither of you has ever tried before, such as a sport, a different kind of restaurant; or learn a new craft together.
- Hike along a path you've never taken before.

How to make love to the same person for the rest of your life

From one man to another
This is a letter from a father to his son on the day before his wedding:

My dear son, Joseph,

You're about to be married. Marriage can be a very wonderful relationship, or it can be terrible. You have the choice to make it as good as it can be, or as bad as it can be. The better husband you are, the better wife you'll have. Treat Ruth badly and she'll only resent you and be angry and want to harm you, too.

Firstly, be committed to her and her only. Let her know that there'll never be anyone else for you, as long as she lives. No affairs, no other women, just Ruth. This will protect your marriage from disease, jealousy and pain, and fill it with trust and love and security.

Give yourself as a gift to your wife, by thinking what Ruth

would most like to receive from you to help her, and make her happy. Give her respect, love, affection, and support, and she'll be more likely to give the same gifts back to you. Take the time to listen to her, and you'll discover what she needs and what will make her happy.

Whenever you have sex, make sure she's ready, comfortable and happy. Put her needs before your own, and she'll be more likely to want to meet your needs too. Many men have very unsatisfying sex because they don't take the time to help their wives enjoy the experience first.

You'll probably want sex more often than Ruth will, but try to hold back a little for her sake. A woman is excited sexually by spending time with a loving husband, who's done something to help her in the day, who's listened to her, appreciated her and touched her gently. The more you help her to feel like a beautiful and sexy woman, the more beautiful and sexy she will become for you. Be considerate when you know she's tired or sad, or in pain, or her day has been difficult. At times like that she needs closeness and comfort without sex. When you have sex together, do only what is acceptable and enjoyable for both of you. Don't just try to have your own needs met, or make Ruth feel uncomfortable. Each of you needs to feel loved and cared for during the experience.

Whatever you do needs to be pleasurable. Whenever something isn't pleasurable, Ruth will be less likely to want it to happen again. She'll be more likely to avoid a similar experience in the future because she'll be afraid of discomfort and pain. Make sure she enjoys everything you do to show your love for her. Sex needs to be enjoyable for both of you. If

it's not, then you need to think why. Make it so good for her that she will beg you for more!
Value each other, honouring each other during the day and the night.
Encourage Ruth with appreciation and gratitude wherever you can, for what she does in the home, and for what she does to

show her love for you. Thank her for the pleasure that making love to her gives you. In private, talk about what helps each of you to enjoy your sexual relationship, and teach each other how to show the best love.

Remember that some sex is wonderful, and some is boring and most of it is somewhere in between. Don't expect it to be perfect every time. Sex is not about perfect technique; it's about perfect love. Be gentle with each other, relax, enjoy your love and laugh about the times when things don't work out perfectly.

Don't do anything that will embarrass Ruth. Your physical relationship together is your own special secret, not to be shared with others. Keep it special. Sometimes you may feel desperate to have your sexual needs met. You may feel like demanding sex. But remember, son, you don't have to have sex every time your body feels like it! No man ever died because he didn't have sex!

I don't have much to give you for a wedding present, but I hope that these few tips will help to give you a special gift that will last a lifetime.

All my love,

Dad.

From one woman to another

My dear daughter, Ruth,

You're about to be married. Marriage can be a very wonderful relationship, or it can be a difficult struggle. You can choose to make your marriage the best that you can. The more acceptance and understanding you show to Joseph, the more acceptance and understanding he is likely to show to you. Treat Joseph well, help him to feel good about himself, and he'll feel good about you, too.

Firstly, be committed to him for as long as you live. No affairs, no other men, just Joseph. This will protect your marriage from disease, jealousy and pain, and fill it with trust and love and security.

Give yourself as a gift to your husband, by thinking what Joseph would most like to receive from you to help him, and make him happy. Give him respect, love, affection, and support, and he'll be more likely to give the same gifts back to you. Take the time to listen to him, and to make him feel like the most special man in the whole world, and you'll discover what he needs to encourage him and strengthen him along the journey of his life.

Remember that sex is a gift from God. It is his idea and it's a very good idea. My mother told me that the angels in heaven clap their hands for joy when a happily married couple enjoy being one flesh together!

Plan times for sex, anticipate and prepare for yourself for them, be relaxed and take plenty of time. Offer sex as often as you feel able to. Offer him sex even when he isn't asking for it. Appeal to his senses by looking, sounding, feeling, tasting and smelling as good as you can. Adore and admire him. When you have sex together, discover your own unique way to enjoy each other. Each of you needs to feel loved and cared for during the experience. Tell him when he does something that makes you feel especially wonderful.

Whatever you do needs to be pleasurable. Sex needs to be enjoyable for both of you. If it's not, then you need to talk about it and find a different way together. Teach each other how to show the best love. Make it so good for him that he will beg you for more!

Value each other, honouring each other during the day and the night. Encourage Joseph with appreciation and gratitude wherever you can, for the things he does to support you, for all the hours he puts in at work, and for keeping your home and car well maintained. Thank him for the pleasure that making love to him gives to you.

Remember that some sex is wonderful, and some is boring and most of it is somewhere in between. If it's not that great tonight, maybe it will be amazing in a few days time. Sex is not about perfect technique; it's about perfect love. Be gentle with each other, relax, enjoy your love and laugh about the times when things don't work out perfectly. Remember that real life sex is quite different from anything you may have seen on the television or in the movies. God gave sex as a wedding gift for both of you. Take it, unwrap it, open the box and discover all its delights.

Have a wonderful wedding, and a great marriage!
All my love,
Mother.

Joseph and Ruth were very fortunate. Their parents had already discovered many of the secrets of successful sex. Joseph had grown up in a home where he saw these positive attitudes lived out between his father and mother everyday.

Putting things right again

But some of us have already made many mistakes along the way, and have all kinds of painful experiences and memories. How can we start to put things right again?

- We may need to apologise to our spouse, however strange that may feel, and show we're genuinely sorry for the mistakes we've made in the past.
- We can show that we're willing to change, and that we want to learn a new way to love each other.
- We can listen to what our spouse will need from us to begin to rebuild the relationship.
- It's important to remember that there are differences between men and women. Men usually desire sex more frequently, and enjoy sexual play and variety, whereas women usually enjoy the emotional sense of being together, feeling close, being touched tenderly, and having more consistent lovemaking techniques.
- Understanding that husbands and wives are different, and taking the time to try and meet the other person's needs, are big steps towards growing closer together sexually.

- We were made to be different to help us explore our relationships, to encourage us to take the time to communicate with each other, and to work together to find ways to help the other person to be happy.
- It's good when we share our hopes and fears about the sexual side of our relationship. This may be difficult if we've not learned to talk about our sexual feelings, but talking about what we like and appreciate about our sexual relationship together can be easier than talking about our difficulties.
- Take it in turns to share one good thing about your lovemaking, and try to build those positive experiences into your times together.
- Talk about your fears about sex too, when you feel able, and then do all you can to take away your spouse's fears about rejection, pain, pregnancy or discomfort.

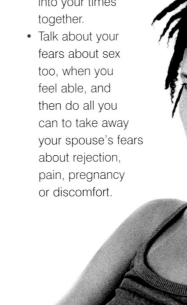

A Good Sex Guide

(Adapted from 1 Corinthians 13:4-8.)

- Love is patient; it doesn't rush the loved one.
- Love is kind; it treats the beloved gently, and makes sure that the he or she feels safe and comfortable.
- Love does not envy the physical appearance of those outside the relationship, or envy the sexual experiences of others.
- Love does not boast about its achievements, but boosts the beloved's confidence, and her picture of herself.
- Love is not proud, it doesn't demand things from the beloved, or try to gain power over him or her, because perfect love casts out fear.
- Love is not self-seeking, but seeks to find new ways to delight the beloved one, and to help him feel completely loved.
- Love is not easily angered, but takes the time to soothe and relax the beloved.
- Love keeps no record of wrongs; there's never any reminding of past failures, or resentment about any mistakes.
- Love always protects the loved one from pain and discomfort.
- Love always trusts, and is worthy of trust, remaining faithful to the relationship at all times.
- Love always hopes that the sexual experience will continue to deepen as intimacy grows with love and understanding.
- Love always perseveres in discovering how the beloved prefers to be loved.
- Love never fails to keep on loving.

For the difficult times

- Sexual relationships often encounter problems. If you are facing a problem, remember that many other people do too.
- It's important to get some help as soon as a problem arises. The longer a difficulty is left without being addressed, the longer it may take to solve the problem.
- Read a reliable book about sexuality. It may answer some of your questions.
- Retrace your steps and start courting each other again, without placing any demands on each other for sex. Take it slowly and see if you can rediscover each other.
- Many problems associated with sex are often the result of overtiredness and stress, so find ways to rest and relax.
- Continue to enjoy other aspects of your relationship and have plenty of non-sexual touching, such as hugs, gentle kisses, caresses, closeness and massage.
- If something doesn't work for you, try something different. It doesn't mean it won't ever work for you, it just means that now isn't the best time.
- Many problems have simple answers and a talk with your family doctor can be helpful.

Love Menus

- Often husbands and wives find it difficult to discuss their ideas about their physical relationship.
- A love menu is just one way to make it easier to explore each other's dreams and ideas about an ideal sexual encounter.
- Take a piece of paper and write on it your own love menu.

Write out your menu under the following headings:

'Restaurant'

Where would you like this 'meal' to take place? (Obviously not in a real restaurant!) What kind of environment would you like? (Candles, fragrances, music, etc.)

'Dress code'

What would you like each of you to wear?

'Appetisers'

What kinds of things would you like to do first? What would make you hungry for more?

'Main course'

Describe the different things that you would find most satisfying and enjoyable.

'Dessert'

What are the things that you like to do afterwards?

'Extras'

Are there any other things that would make the love menu really special for you? For example, where do you most like to be touched? Are there any treats you would like to have?

How to use the love menus

- Once you have both written your menus, swap them with each other and create a special experience for your spouse.
- You can choose the things you would like to do from the menu that they are offering you.
- Take it in turns to choose ideas from the other's menu.
- Show appreciation to each other by expressing what you most enjoyed about each love feast, and learn more about delighting in each other.

Wedding anniversary ideas

- Have a special prayer that you pray for each other on your anniversaries. Perhaps it could be based on a prayer that was said during your wedding, or you could write your own.
- Read 1 Corinthians 13 together and think of ways you could be kinder, and more patient and unselfish to each other, etc.
- Invite your children to a special meal in your home. Cook a celebration dinner and wear the clothes you wore on your wedding day, if possible. Show your children any photos and mementoes from the day. Let them know how much you still love each other.
- Tell your children five things that attracted you to your spouse.
- Let your children help to create anniversary cards and gifts for each of you.
- Attend a marriage enrichment retreat if there is one in your area. These are designed for couples who care about their marriages, and give you a special time away to think about your relationship and appreciate the good things you share together.
- Buy a good Christian book on marriage as an anniversary gift for you both, and read it through the coming year.
- Go back to where you first met, or where something special happened during your courtship, and recreate those special memories, taking a picnic, or eating out in a nearby restaurant.
- Evaluate the past year. Look for ways in which your relationship has grown and been strengthened, and thank God and each other for those things. Ask God to help you make plans and goals for your relationship that he will help you to achieve in the year ahead.

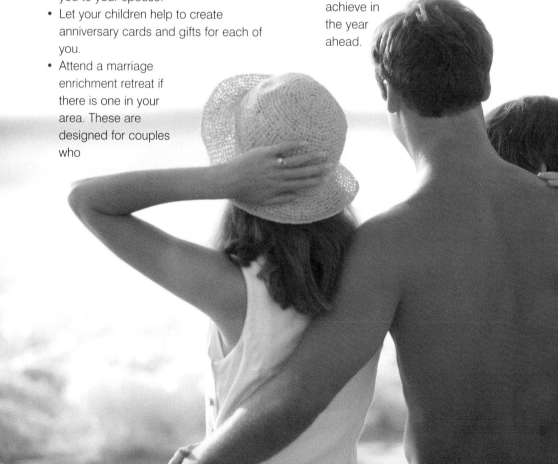

Strengthening the marriages around you

What makes a strong marriage?
- Being able to laugh together.
- Coming to value your differences as strengths rather than irritants.
- Creating happy memories together.
- Giving both of you a safe place to talk about your ideas and feelings, and your hopes and fears.
- Managing conflicts without letting them escalate out of control.
- Being able to offer and ask for forgiveness.
- Solving problems quickly by negotiating the best solution for both of you.
- Learning all you can about how to build a strong marriage.
- Making your marriage a high priority, so that you avoid taking on responsibilities and jobs that will have a negative impact on your relationship.
- Having a couple who can mentor you through the ups and downs of married life.
- Understanding how much God loves you and what his love really means, so that you are better able to love your spouse.
- Praying together and finding creative ways to worship and study the Bible together.
- Valuing each other's strengths, and appreciating each other.
- Discovering what you can do to help your husband or wife to feel really loved.

Strengthening your own marriage
- Celebrate your marriage every day in small, but thoughtful and creative ways. Tell each other how glad you are to be married, delight in each other and find ways to show each other kindness, appreciation, affection and support.
- Make it a goal to attend a marriage retreat annually. If there are none in your area, see if you could get a group together who could invite a couple to your area to lead out in a retreat.
- Find a good book about marriage and buy two copies. Read a chapter each week on your own, and then think of three questions you would like to ask your husband or

wife about what you have read. Meet weekly to discuss your ideas. Pass the books to other couples when you have finished with them. Or start a book circle to pass pairs of books around a group of married couples.

- Try out lots of unusual ways to have fun together! Laugh, share happy memories, and just enjoy being together. Try *40 Unforgettable Dates with your Mate* by Dr Gary and Barbara Rosberg (ISBN 0-8423-6106-5), or buy a *Simply Romantic Nights* kit from *www.familylife.com*.
- Subscribe to a magazine that strengthens marriage. *Marriage Partnership* magazine is an excellent publication. View sample articles and archives online at *www.marriagepartnership.com*. Give gift subscriptions to the magazine as wedding presents. Forward useful articles from the website to your friends.
- Have regular weekly meetings to co-ordinate diaries, make financial plans, organise family schedules, etc. to take care of the little details of married life.
- Discover how each of you prefers to be loved. Write a list for each other of the times when you felt very loved by your husband or wife, and look for themes. Talk about other things that would help you to feel special and loved, and listen to the ways in which you could share your love in the future. Keep on talking about your preferences and needs, as they may change from time to time. Don't expect your husband or wife to guess what you need.

- Sign up for creative ways to 'romance' each other at *www.familylife.com*. You can sign up for ideas for him, or ideas for her, and each of you will be sent an idea twice a week.
- Talk together about your hopes for your marriage. Make plans to turn these hopes into realities.
- Run a small group seminar for couples in your own home. Use ready-made videos and materials to make it easy for you, and invite three or four couples to join you. Visit *www.2-in-2-1.co.uk* for ideas for resources, or download the HomeBuilders Couples

Series from *www.familylife.com*. For British materials use *The Marriage Course* from Holy Trinity Brompton, 'Time for Each Other' from CPO, 'Keeping Marriages Healthy' from Intimate Life Ministries and 'The Marriage Toolkit' from Care for the Family.

- Pray for your own marriage and each other everyday. Consider how much God loves you both, and find ways to show your husband or wife how much they are loved by God.

Strengthening the marriages of family and friends

- Write letters of appreciation to couples who have inspired and strengthened your marriage, or design a card for this purpose on your computer. Encourage other couples to do the same.
- Celebrate the anniversaries of your family and friends in a special way. Hold a surprise party, send cards, and give marriage-building books. Show them that their marriage is important to you, too.
- Sign up for an email service that offers weekly marriage strengthening tips and forward these ideas to family and friends at *www.2-in-2-1.co.uk*.
- Pass around an attractive blank book at a wedding reception and invite people to write their favourite marriage 'date' ideas, and any tips they would like to share to strengthen the couple's marriage.
- During wedding services, have a special moment of recommitment for the married couples who are attending.
- Invite other couples to come together for fun, either for a meal at your home, or a picnic, or to go bowling, etc. Many couples don't take the time to have fun in their relationship, so this may encourage them to relax together.

- Invite couples around to watch a marriage strengthening video such as *The Story of Us*, *A Beautiful Mind*, *Family Man* and *Town and Country*. Create some discussion questions for the couples to take home and discuss together. Visit *www.smartmarriages.com* for an excellent discussion guide for *The Story of Us*. Give marriage strengthening books, videos and tapes as engagement, wedding, birth, anniversary and birthday gifts.
- Encourage married couples who are experiencing a long-distance relationship to visit *www.longdistancecouples.com* for creative ideas about strengthening a relationship where the husband and wife have to live apart because of work commitments, etc.
- Offer to provide babysitting, or have your friends' children sleep at your home for the night, so that couples can go out together and have some time alone.

The marriages of those in your church community

- Plan an annual marriage retreat for your church congregation. Choose a good venue – some hotels can offer cheaper deals at weekends and provide leisure facilities too. Invite an experienced couple to lead the retreat, or use prepared marriage seminars. See list of resources on page 173.
- Avoid giving too many church-related jobs to one

family. Where possible, encourage the husband and wife to work together in a shared ministry so that the church doesn't pull couples apart.
- Take care of the marriages of your church leaders. Help them to be accountable for spending time with their families. Pay for them to attend a marriage retreat at least every couple of years.
- Encourage your church leaders to preach about marriage regularly, at least once a year during National Marriage Week (the week containing 14 February), but preferably more often.
- Make sure that every couple about to be married in your church is well prepared for marriage.
  - Encourage your church to honour those who have been married for a long time. Hold a party, or send the couple on a weekend marriage retreat, or short break away.
  - In a large church, hold monthly or quarterly anniversary parties for all the couples who have had an anniversary during that time period. It doesn't have to be elaborate, just a drink and cake, or cheese and biscuits, or coffee and dessert. Play couple games, watch a marriage strengthening video together, or share happy marriage memories.
  - Invite the teenagers in your church to compile a booklet of

marriage-strengthening ideas. Encourage them to interview some of the married couples in the congregation as they research this booklet. Provide good relationship education for teens in the church.

- Hold marriage banquets in your church, or arrange for a banquet at a local hotel. If you choose a buffet-style dinner this may not be very expensive. Invite speakers for after-dinner marriage speeches, mini-seminars, or even to act out marriage-strengthening sketches!
- Start a marriage strengthening resource library at your church. Include good video packages, such as the *Time for Each Other* kits from CPO, *Sixty Minute Marriage* from Care for the Family, and other materials listed in the Resource section.
- Designate one day a week as a special day to pray for marriages – your own marriages, those of your family and friends, those of your congregations and church leadership, and the marriages of community leaders and policy makers.
- Make sure that your church has a sign directing couples to Christian counsellors who are skilled at working with marriages, so that those facing difficulties know where to turn.
- Hold a special prayer breakfast for couples. Serve a delicious breakfast at tables for two, and give each couple a 'menu' of creative prayer ideas. Allow some space and time for couple prayer as well as group prayer.
- Whenever your church puts on events for married couples, be sure to arrange adequate child care so that as many can attend as possible, having the childcare in the same building as the event can be especially helpful to parents of young

babies and mothers who are breastfeeding.

Strengthening marriages in your workplace

- Talk to your employer about the benefits of workers who have happy marriages and help raise awareness of the need to invest in the marriages of employees. Visit *www.smartmarriages.com* for examples of research to support your case.
- Ask your employer to honour wedding

anniversaries by offering an extra day of leave on wedding anniversaries. Or perhaps by sending a bouquet to the couple, or a gift voucher for a cinema or restaurant. Encourage your employer to arrange social events for the whole family to attend. At work parties and banquets have a time when the husbands and wives of workers are honoured and thanked.

- If you find out when your colleagues are having their wedding anniversaries, send a card, or email them about websites that have marriage-strengthening ideas or tips for romance.
- Offer to run lunch-time marriage-strengthening courses in the workplace, or show clips of the video *Sixty Minute Marriage* by Rob Parsons, from Care for the Family. Hand out discussion cards for employees to take home and discuss with their spouses.
- If your employer puts extra pressure on the workforce to work long hours, challenge the practice and encourage work patterns that support marriages and families, instead of those that add extra stresses to relationships. Help the employer to see that when his employees have happy marriages and families, he will have a happier, healthier, and more productive work-force.

Strengthening the marriages of those in your local community

- Invite your congregation to offer regular baby-sitting at the church so that parents can go on dates together. This could also be offered as a service to your local community. Consider Saturday or Sunday afternoons/evenings. Parents need to pre-book places so that you have enough helpers. Children can bring their own

packed tea and the church can provide care and play for the little ones and a programme of activity for the older children. Your helpers must have all been police-checked to ensure that they have no criminal records, and that they are trained in child protection and safety.

- Talk to head teachers about the benefits to pupils when their parents have happy marriages, Find research at *www.smartmarriages.com* to help support your case. Invite the school to help sponsor an event to strengthen the parents' marriages.
- Choose one of the activities in this section and put it into action during National

Marriage Week. (Remember – February 14th.) For more ideas and information about National Marriage Week visit *www.nmw.org.uk*.
- Sponsor a contest in your local paper. Free papers may be especially open to your ideas. Invite people to write 200 words starting with the line, 'I'm happy to be married because . . .' Ask the paper to print the winning ones, and offer the prize of a restaurant voucher, theatre voucher or weekend break for the winner, and marriage-strengthening books for winner and runners up. You may be able to negotiate with restaurants, hotels and book shops to donate the prizes.
- Encourage health visitors and others providing antenatal classes to include a session for couples to help them strengthen their marriage as they enter parenthood.
- Ask your local library to provide a list of the marriage-strengthening books they hold. Often you can request that your library provides specific books, and you may be able to persuade them to purchase more books to loan.
- Sponsor a float at the local carnival. Create a design to show the value of marriage and hand out marriage-strengthening leaflets along the way.
- Make a marriage-strengthening display and ask your local library if you can set it up for a fixed time period. Try for National Marriage Week. Include leaflets for people to take away, and advertise marriage strengthening events. If you have any friends who are skilled at graphics and display, ask them to help you.
- Create posters to encourage people to work on their marriages, Work with any graphic designers that you know. Be creative with your computer publishing programme. Small posters could be placed in buses, libraries, surgeries, public notice boards, etc.
- Sponsor a writing competition at your local school. Set a subject like 'How to have a happy marriage'. Offer prizes that will appeal to the age of the children in the school. Perhaps you could offer vouchers

for the whole family to have a special outing to a local theme park.

- If you are a higher education teacher maybe you could offer to teach an evening class in strengthening marriages. Use pre-prepared materials to help you.

People you meet

- When chatting with strangers, invite them to tell you their marriage-strengthening ideas. You can tell them that you are collecting them for a booklet or leaflet. If they are interested, take their details and send them a copy of the finished product. Ask people in conversation to share their happiest marriage memories, or best marriage date ideas.
- Carry leaflets and even helpful books about marriage to give to people you meet.

Using the media to help strengthen marriages

- Ask your local radio station to run a competition for the most creative ideas for a low-budget date for a married couple.
- Write letters to the editor of your local paper praising any community effort to strengthen marriages and pointing out the harm that can be done by any policies undermining marriage. Always be courteous and polite in the letter-writing.
- Ask your local *Yellow Pages* if they could include some marriage-strengthening tips in their empty advertising spots. You will need to give them a list of short tips to include. If necessary, be willing to sponsor adverts close to Counselling, Marriage and Wedding listings.
- When you see a television programme that offers a positive picture of marriage, write and thank the producer. If you seen an advert or programme that portrays a

negative picture of marriage, write and share your views in a polite manner. Use statistics to help support your case and do all you can to encourage producers and presenters to give marriage good publicity.

- Offer to write a regular feature of marriage-building ideas for your local paper. Talk to the editor about the word count he requires and show samples of your articles.
- Encourage your local paper to run feature articles on couples who have been married a long time.
- Write to 'agony columns' telling positive stories of how marriage education and mentoring has helped your marriage.
- Make a list of ten exciting 'dates' for married couples in your area. Publish them in your local paper or make them into a leaflet to leave in the information centre, libraries, etc.*

* for resources on this section go to page 173

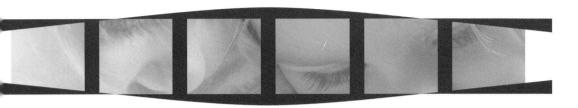

Chapter 5
Facing life's challenges together

Coping with the tough times

Tough times happen. This is a difficult world to live in. There are famines, droughts, wars, pests, dangers, illnesses, disappointments and death. It's not easy to deal with the difficult times. They can challenge our families to the limits. Sometimes we may feel like giving up because life seems too difficult to manage.

Each of us faces different challenges in life. A challenge that you face easily may seem impossible for me to face. One thing is certain in an uncertain world, and that is when we face challenges *together* we are often stronger, and the experience brings us closer together.

How can you help your family face the big and little challenges in life?
- Firstly, look out for signs that someone in the family is struggling with a situation. When someone is hurting, be sensitive to his or her different needs. We may feel that they just need to grow up and manage their feelings on their own, but when people have to face challenges without sympathy, they can learn to lose sympathy for others, too.
- Look out for those who suddenly want to be alone, look sad, don't want to eat, or who seem to find everything about life too much to cope with. A child may not want to go to school because he is being bullied or teased there, but he may pretend to be ill instead, so that he doesn't have to admit that he's being bullied. Find out what is causing the unusual behaviour.

- Accept the feelings of the struggling person, and don't minimise those feelings or tease the person. Let him know it's all right to cry, even if he is a boy, or a man. Humans were made with eyes that cry, and tears can cleanse the heart of all kinds of hurts. Feelings aren't good or bad – feelings just are. We can't always control our feelings, just as we can't control our heart-beat, or our digestion. Crying can be very helpful in soothing a distressed mind or body, so let the tears flow freely.

- Take the time to listen to one another and understand the *unspoken* communication so that you can tell when someone is upset or afraid even if he or she can't find the words or the courage to tell you.

- Show comfort for someone by using appropriate affection, such as touches, hugs, kind words and gentleness. Physical contact with other

'Praise be to the God and Father of our Lord Jesus Christ, the Father of compassion and the God of all comfort, who comforts us in all our troubles, so that we can comfort those in any trouble with the comfort we ourselves have received from God.'
2 Corinthians 1:3, 4.

'And surely I am with you always, to the very end of the age.' Matthew 28:20.

human beings can be very comforting at a distressing time. Touch can be reassuring when we're afraid, soothing when we're stressed and even healing when we're hurt.

- Encourage the distressed person to talk to you, by showing that you care and that you can be trusted. When he talks, listen well, and concentrate on what he has to say. Put yourself in his situation for a while and think how it must feel. Say things like, 'That must have been very distressing for you . . .' 'You must have been very frightened then . . .' or 'I think I would have felt like that, too.' If someone shares a secret with you, ask their permission if you need to tell someone else what was said.

- If someone in your family is suffering, make spending time together your top priority. Show, in lots of ways, that his/her needs are important to you. Don't wait for things to get better naturally. They probably will, but in the meantime it will be much better if you're there to help take away fears, comfort tears and deal with resentments.

- Be honest about how much you can do to help. You're not perfect and you can't be there all the time, but you do care. If you have been part of the original hurt, be willing to ask for forgiveness. Admit your failures and your fears, even as a parent. Your children will know your weak points anyway, and will respect you for being honest about them. Children need to know that you're not perfect, and that you don't expect them to be perfect all the time either.

- When there's a physical calamity, such as flood, famine, drought, or crop failure, we're often powerless to help ourselves. We can just hope and pray that people will come to help us and bring us what we need. In those situations we can feel very vulnerable because there is so little we can do to help ourselves.

- Help the person who is struggling to find a way to forgive the source of the hurt, if forgiveness is needed. Those who are eventually able to forgive a deep hurt will usually cope with the difficult situation better than those who let resentments build up. But forgiveness for a great hurt can take a long time, so sometimes we need to be

'Encourage the timid, help the weak, be patient with everyone.'
1 Thessalonians 5:14.

patient and not rush anyone into forgiving another person until he or she is ready.

- Think of all the positive things that can come out of the difficult situation. Sit down together and say anything that comes to mind that might be positive about the situation. When locusts ate Lennie's crops, his family enjoyed trying to catch the locusts because in their culture deep-fried locusts were a special treat. Then some aid workers came to his area to teach the farmers good farming skills. They trained Lennie to teach the other farmers, paid him for his work and even provided food for the family.

- You could try to find a way to do something good for a person who has caused you hurt. This may sound unusual, but it can have dramatic and positive effects. Sometimes the most hurtful people are those for whom no one has ever done anything nice. King Solomon once said that a gift given in secret could soothe an angry heart, and open up closed doors.

- When you're facing a difficult situation with your family, use wisdom, listen to others who've faced similar circumstances, and talk together about the best decision to follow.

- If the whole family is facing

a difficult time, stay close together to comfort and support one another. Let them know that they're loved and special and that you're doing your best to take care of their needs, even if you can't put everything right.

• When the tough times come, as tough times will, use them to bring your family closer together, spend time with them, notice their feelings and help them to talk about their fears and their sorrows. That's real strength.

> 'Like one who takes away a garment on a cold day, or like vinegar poured on soda, is one who sings songs to a heavy heart.'
> Proverbs 25:20.

Soothing each other

People who study healthy relationships have found that one of the secrets of a strong and happy relationship is the ability to soothe each other when there is distress, sadness or pain.

Debbie, Jay and the difficult day

As soon as Jay came through the front door, Debbie knew he'd had a hard day. His face was tight and tired-looking. His shoulders sagged. He let his bag drop to the floor. His whole body looked heavy, and he sat heavily in the chair and held his head. Jay didn't have such days very often, but they happened perhaps once or twice a month. Debbie had learned to be quiet and not bother him for a while when he came through the door looking like that. She tiptoed away and went to make him his favourite drink. She served it with a piece of his favourite cake. It was her way of silently saying, I care about what you're going through right now, and I hurt for you.

In a little while, when he'd had some quiet space, she'd serve him his favourite food. She'd help him with his chores. They'd go for a short walk and talk about their day. Then she'd pour some oil on her hands and give him a back massage to help him relax before he went to sleep.

Freda and George – Being there

Freda was very sad. She'd never been so sad in her whole life. Her mother had just died and it felt to her as if the whole world had become bleak and lonely. George had never seen his wife so sad before. She seemed to be crying all the time. He wanted to show

how much he cared, but he didn't know how. He felt so sad, too, seeing her like that. He sat with her whenever he could, and held her hand, just so she could feel he was near her. He didn't know what to say to comfort her, so he just said, 'I'm sorry that you hurt so badly and I want you to know that I'm here with you, and I'll be here with you as long as it takes to help you feel better.'

Helping her cry

Little Tina came home late from school.

'Where have you been, Tina?' her mum asked.

'I've been with Lisa. You see Lisa dropped her best doll, and it broke, and I stayed to help her.'

'Oh, you stayed to help her fix the doll. That was kind of you, Tina.'

'No mum, I couldn't fix the doll, so I stayed to help her cry.'

Comforting the cut

Jerry came crying to his dad. He'd fallen down on some sharp stones and his leg was bleeding. To a young boy, it seemed as if there was lots of blood. He was scared, and he hurt badly, too. Dad picked him up and held him close, as he carried him to the house, bathed his knee clean, wrapped it in a clean bandage and then used his pen to draw a funny face on the bandage over the cut. Jerry began to smile again. Dad found Jerry a drink, and sat on the steps outside with him for a few minutes, telling him a story. Soon Jerry was up and running around again.

Soothing and comforting

- There are times in our lives when we need some comfort, when we need to be soothed. Some of the best relationships are those where each person knows how to soothe the other, and knows how to help the other calm down and feel better again.
- Different cultures may have different ways to show comfort and concern, and to be soothed. In some places drinks are soothing, a hot cup of herbal tea, or a refreshing glass of cold water. Some show

'Laugh with your happy friends when they're happy; share tears when they're down.'
Romans 12:15, The Message.

comfort by bringing flowers, or using special music. For some people being with the sad person is the important thing to do.

- Just as different cultures have different ways to be soothed, each of us is different, and we all have special ways in which we like to be comforted.

> 'Praise be to the God and Father of our Lord Jesus Christ . . . who comforts us in all our troubles, so that we can comfort those in any trouble with the comfort we ourselves have received from God.'
>
> 2 Corinthians 1:3,4.

The two things we need to know

- Comforting is not about trying to make the other person happy.
- When someone is sad, he is sad. If you try to make him feel happy, he may feel that you don't understand his pain. If you try to make him forget his sadness, or try to persuade him that the thing he's being sad about is really only small, he will also feel misunderstood, because the pain feels very big to him. Responding in these ways can make the person who is sad feel even more isolated in his pain.
- When we're having a difficult time, we usually need two things:
    1 We need to know that we're not alone in our sadness because someone is there with us.
    2 We need to know that the person who is with us is trying to understand what we're experiencing.
- If we feel that there's no one there to be with us, we can feel very alone, and this can increase our sadness.
- If we feel that our pain isn't accepted and understood, then this can also make us feel more miserable.
- When we experience togetherness and

understanding, we're more likely to feel comforted.

When might we need comfort?

- Think of the some of the times when you feel you need comforting.
- When we're sick and ill we need the comfort of knowing someone is there to take care of us, and that she'll do all she can to help us to feel better. Maybe she'll bring a cool cloth for our hot head, or make some good soup for us when we don't feel like eating much.
- Disappointments need comfort too: When we fail an exam, or when we don't get a job that we wanted; when our crop fails and the bad weather comes and spoils our homes – we need comfort. We may need someone to be there with us to share our feeling of loss, and, when the time is right, to give us hope again.
- When someone we love has died, we need comforting because our loss is so very great. If we lose a crop, it's hard, but maybe next year will be better. When we lose people we love, we may feel as if we

have lost them forever, even if our faith and culture tells us a different story.

- Sometimes we have a bad day. We may feel misunderstood, used, abused, exhausted and challenged, and we need a loving person to bring us comfort and soothe our troubled minds and bodies.
- Sometimes we have hurt, or been hurt by, someone we love, and this can make us sad. At these times we need to find each other again and offer comfort, so that the relationship can be healed.

Thinking about it

- Think about the times when you needed comfort. Who gave it to you? What did they do? What did you like about what they did? What wasn't so helpful? Maybe there wasn't anyone to comfort you. If so, you'll be able to understand even more how lonely it feels to be sad when you don't have a comforting person to be there with you.
- Is there someone you know right now who may need comforting? Think first about those most closely related to you: your spouse, and your children, and the family where you grew up. Who needs

comforting? Do you know how they like to be comforted? If not, you can ask them, and they'll probably appreciate your interest in their lives. You won't feel so uneasy about what to do if you know the special way that someone likes to be soothed and comforted.

- This is a troubled world. It's not easy to live here. There's lots of pain and disappointment. But some soothing moments and some caring comfort, can bring a little peace into a hurting heart.

Comforting ideas

- Have a special comforting blanket or sheet. Whenever anyone feels sad they can wrap themselves in the blanket and other family members can come and hug them. Make this blanket look different from the other blankets in your home, or choose one that is soft and fluffy.
- Place a flower on the pillow of someone's bed. Choose lavender or other fragrant flowers that may bring refreshment and relaxation.
- Make a special drink for someone who needs comforting and serve it in an attractive way.
- Put a note in work or school bags when someone is having a hard time, or if he has an exam to do, to let him know you're thinking of him, and that you care about the challenges he has to face.
- When someone has died, give time for family and friends to talk about the person they have lost, and their special memories.
- Make regular contact with someone who is hurting, so that he or she doesn't feel so isolated. If possible, leave flowers or other small gifts to show that you care, even though you can't be there.

Beating the bullies

Tom – bullied for being small

Tom's life was miserable. He was shorter than average for his age and the taller boys in his class picked on him and taunted him. They never did it in front of the teacher. It was always in a quiet, but hurtful, comment as they passed him in the corridor, or in a note slipped into his book. Their cruel words were engraved on his mind, making him feel humiliated, angry and worthless.

Kate – teased for working hard

Kate was a good student. She did well in all her subjects. It looked as if she would really excel in her school exams. But suddenly her grades began to slip, and she became quiet and sad. No one knew that some of her classmates were teasing her, calling her Teacher's Pet, ridiculing her for working hard, and threatening to beat her up if she continued to get good marks.

Ben – racial bullying

Ben worked for four years after he left school. Every day he was racially bullied. Finally he couldn't cope any more. The suicide note blamed his workmates for his death.

About bullying

• Bullying comes in all kinds of shapes and sizes. It can be hitting and kicking, and threatening to hurt. It can be calling names, spreading untrue rumours, and sending hurtful notes. It can be racially motivated, it can be because someone is jealous, or it can be just because someone looks or

behaves a little differently.
- Bullying is dangerous. It can be life-threatening. It's very hard for a bully to understand the effect of the bullying behaviour on a victim. Bullying can cause depression, low self-esteem, loneliness, poor school work, and even threatened or attempted suicide.
- Bullying is always wrong. People have a right to be treated with respect and equality, and to live their lives safe from the threat of harm.

Helping someone who is being bullied
- Firstly, believe what they say and take the time to listen carefully to their story.
- Find out exactly what has happened, when, how, by whom and to what extent.
- By sharing their story with you, they have already crushed some of the bully's power.
- Praise them for doing the right thing and telling you.
- Reassure them that the bullying is not their fault.
- Let them know that in order to help them you may have to talk to someone else, like a teacher or doctor.
- Make sure that the school provides good anti-bullying training for all of the teachers.
- Check the school's policy on bullying and explain it to the victim, so that he or she feels safe about telling the school.
- Help the child to feel loved and cared for by you.
- Bullies want their victims to suffer alone; don't let them have this pleasure.
- Reassure the child that you will do everything in your power to help them feel safe, even if it means going to a new school, or staying away from school for a time. This may make your life difficult, but the child needs to know that you will protect them at all costs.
- Help them to avoid potential bullying situations, such as on the way to and from school, by finding a different way of getting to school.
- Teach your child to say 'No' firmly and to walk away from the bullying where possible. Bullies like to know they have scared others, so help your child to act

confidently, and as if the bully doesn't bother them. Find ways to answer the bully's taunts in a firm, perhaps humorous way that will disarm the bully.

'Defend the cause of the weak and fatherless; maintain the rights of the poor and oppressed. Rescue the weak and needy; deliver them from the hand of the wicked.'
Psalm 82:3, 4.

• Find positive things they can do that will encourage their self-esteem and help them to feel good about themselves again.

Helping a bully

• Bullying is never acceptable, but sometimes the bully may also be a victim and in need of special help. Bullying is not a good pattern for life. Many prison inmates admitted to

having been bullies when they were young.

• Often bullies feel powerless in their own lives and bullying others is a way for them to feel in control, especially if they have experienced bereavement, or divorce, or feel inadequate themselves.

• Ask the bully if he or she has any ideas why they might be choosing to bully others.

• Help them to feel loved and cared for, and to find something positive so that they can feel good about themselves.

• Explore ways in which the bully can make amends for the bullying.

• Reward good behaviour.

• Teach positive skills for relating to others.

• Channel their energies into creative, constructive or energetic activities.

Beating the bully is something we all need to do. Every time we treat someone with care and respect, we are helping to immunise them against bullying or being bullied, whether they are an adult or a child.

Helping a child who is playing truant

Thousands of children miss school every day, and their parents don't even know what they are doing. This is called playing truant. In some countries truancy is illegal and parents can be prosecuted and face heavy fines, which can be taken directly from their wages. Some parents may even have to give up their jobs to help make sure that their children get to school.

The best ways to reduce truancy are usually where both the school and the family are working together to support the child. Parents who take a special interest in their children's education, and show that they value learning, can help to reduce the risk of children playing truant.

A teenager missing a day from school doesn't seem such a big thing. And maybe it's not. Just one day probably won't make a huge difference to his/her life. But truancy is a major source of concern for some education systems today. Schools may blame the parents for not getting the children to school. The parents may blame the school for not meeting the needs of children. Children may be missing school because they are afraid of someone or something. Some children who are missing school are concerned about a friend who is staying away from school for personal reasons, and they are trying to help them, but may not be quite sure what to do.

'School's boring.' That's what many of the children who play truant give as the reason why they're not

going to school. But there is often a wide variety of reasons. School may even seem irrelevant to some children if their skills and abilities are more practical, and they're not interested in getting any qualifications. The combination of reasons will probably vary from child to child, and day to day.

If you think your child is a truant, you might like to think through some of the following ideas and use whatever seems helpful to your situation:

Take the time to listen to what your child has to say about why he is absent from school. Maybe he will need to know that you're not angry before he will feel free to talk, so providing a place and atmosphere where it's safe to talk can be helpful.

Understand that what your child says will be his or her experience of the situation. Even if you have a different understanding of what might be happening, the child's experience is valid, and

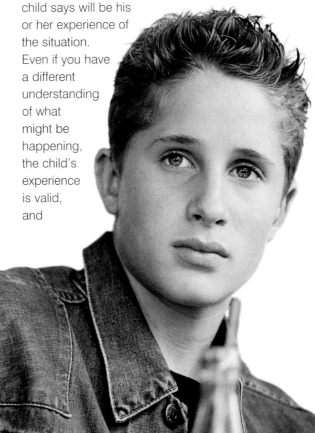

needs to be respected as an important perspective. After all, he is the one who is choosing not to go to school, and that is not always an easy choice to make.

It can help to normalise the experience by expressing that being a truant seems like the best way of dealing with a difficult situation. Ask what your child most fears about going to school, and what he most likes about going to school.

If your child tells you what he fears most, ask how he would like to begin to tackle the fear, and how you might be able to help. Children might be afraid of a teacher, or of public humiliation if a class is too difficult, or maybe they are struggling with reading, or worried about coursework deadlines and exams. Perhaps they are being bullied, or feeling lonely and miserable at school.

If you discover that your child is missing school to try to help another child in difficulty, you might like to praise her for being such a supportive friend, and encourage her to think about other ways to be helpful without having to miss school.

You might like to talk to school personnel and listen to their ideas about your child. Invite the child to tell you what she thinks are the useful things about missing school, and what might be some useful things about going to school.

Ask how you can be helpful to the child. Can you talk to the school on her behalf, or find someone else that your child would be happy to have speaking for her? Involve your child in any plans you make and check any letters or the content of conversations that you plan to have with the school, so that your child feels safe about what you might do.

Talk to the school and explore what the teachers may have been noticing about your child. Listen to the teachers' ideas, remembering that they also have only part of the story. Ask the school or form tutor to call you if your child doesn't come to school, and in return, call the school if your child is not going into school because of illness or medical appointments.

Perhaps you could help your child to realise that truancy is breaking the law by talking about some teenagers you may have seen who were picked up by the police in a local shopping mall, and taken back to school. By telling the story about other children, you may be able to get the message across without sounding as if you are specifically targeting your own child's behaviour.

Think about your life as a parent, and what was happening in the family around the time when the child began to play truant.

- What might have triggered the child's choice to play truant?
- How does your child know that you support him or her?
- How do you show that education is important to you?
- Has learning helped you to achieve your goals in life?
- How does remembering what life was like for you at school help you, or make it more difficult for you, as you talk about truancy with your child?

Finally, have you ever felt like taking a day off work, even though you weren't really ill? How different is that from playing truant? Put yourself in your child's shoes for a while and see if that helps you to see things differently.

Helping a child cope with the loss of a loved one

Death can be bewildering and scary for any one of us, and especially for a child. As a parent you will be experiencing your own sadness and facing different challenges. It may be helpful for you to find other people who can comfort and support you at this time.

Everyone experiences a death in a different way, and children are no exception. The most important thing is to create the space for your child to talk so you can listen to what they are thinking, and you can choose how to respond. It is helpful to accept whatever your child says, and ask simple but open ended questions to give you a fuller understanding of their thoughts.

Here are some practical ideas that may be helpful for you to think about:

- Encourage the child to talk about his or her feelings about the death. Children can feel somehow responsible for causing a death, so it's important to help them to understand why the person died, and reassure them that they didn't do anything to cause the death.
- If possible, let the child attend the funeral. Explain everything that will happen, so that the child can understand and make the choice whether to attend or not. It may be helpful to give the child a special role to play at the funeral, such as flowers to place on the casket, or a short poem to read, but let them choose what to do, and have the freedom not to do it if they change their mind at the last minute.
- Perhaps you could have a book at the funeral in which people can write their special memories of the loved one, or give out slips of paper to people and collect them to stick into a book of memories for family members to read. Friends, colleagues and neighbours may have very different memories of the person, and you may discover some surprises.
- You may be sad too, but don't forget the needs of the child. Perhaps you could make an agreement that the child comes to you when he or she feels especially sad.

One family has a comfort chair, an old

squishy armchair with a soft blanket. Whenever a child is sad, his mother wraps him in the blanket and hugs him till he feels better.

- Help your child make a special collection of memories, in a box, or in a book. Collect photos, stories, cards sent to and from the loved one, a list of presents exchanged, and any special items that represent the relationship, and are meaningful to your child.

- Another idea is to make a small booklet in which each page is a different month of the year. Your child can draw pictures of memories shared at different times, the loved one's birthday, family traditions, sledging in January, a holiday by the sea in July, making a rabbit hutch together in October.

- You may like to choose a day for remembering the special person each year. It could be on their birthday, or the anniversary of their death. Choose activities to do that become a tradition each year. This may be as simple as laying flowers on the grave, or eating their favourite meal, or having a brief memorial service, with some favourite hymns and a short prayer.

- You could plant a tree in memory of your loved one. Your child can choose the tree and help to dig the hole and plant the tree. Take a photo each year of the child next to the tree to see how they both grow.

- At special events, when it feels as if someone special is missing from the gathering, because they've died, you could light a candle in their memory, leave an empty chair, or place flowers or their photograph in the place.

- Let your child choose something from the loved one's belongings, that they can always keep to remind them of the special person. It could be an item of clothing, or a tool, a picture, a piece of furniture, or a cup. Help them to keep it safe.

- Tell your child stories about the life of the person who's died. Maybe you could even write a miniature biography for the child, to fill in the gaps in their memory and give them a fuller picture of the person's life and achievements.

- Some children may like to have a link with the person who died at their special life events. If you find a half-finished tapestry, keep it for a granddaughter to complete when she's older, or finish it yourself, and give it to her made up as a cushion.

Perhaps you can save other things from the loved one's belongings to give to the child at different stages in life, such as a book when starting school, an old diary when reaching the teens, old love letters, or an item of clothing to wear at their wedding, and so on. You could say, 'I think your Grandma would have liked to have given you this today, if she were here.'

- Every child is unique, and every relationship is different. Don't be afraid to ask your child what he or she would like, or thinks should happen. Be sure to let the child know that you are always available to talk about the person who has died, and answer questions. Keep talking and listening to the child, so that you're always ready to help through the stages of grief.

What the Bible says about death:

'And regarding the question, friends, that has come up about what happens to those already dead and buried, we don't want you in the dark any longer. First off, you must not carry on over them like people who have nothing to look forward to, as if the grave were the last word. Since Jesus died and broke loose from the grave, God will most certainly bring back to life those who died in Jesus.

'And then this: We can tell you with complete confidence – we have the Master's word on it – that when the Master comes again to us, those of us who are still alive will (not be ahead) of the dead, and leave them behind. In actual fact, they'll be ahead of us. The Master himself will give the command. Archangel thunder! God's trumpet blast! He'll come down from heaven and the dead in Christ will rise – they'll go first. Then the rest of us who are still alive at the time will be caught up with them into the clouds to meet the Master. Oh, we'll be walking on air! And then there will be one huge family reunion with the Master. So reassure one another with these words.' 1 Thessalonians 4:13-18, The Message.

Help! My family is falling to pieces!

Many families try to stay together, but sometimes this isn't possible. Husbands and wives separate and family relationships break down. For most children this is a traumatic experience, and most parents want to find ways to help their children through this difficult time. Here are some ideas that others have found helpful:

- Help the children to talk about their emotions. They may feel that they have to hide their feelings so that they don't hurt either of the parents. It can be hard for a parent to listen to the difficult feelings of their hurting children, but the children need to know that their feelings are important, and that they won't be judged for having them.
- If you find it hard to open up a discussion

Single parents in the Bible Hagar was a single parent. As a servant girl she gave Abraham his first son, but she was sent away when Abraham's wife had a child in her old age. She took her child and went to find a home in the desert. Just when all hope of finding food and water had disappeared, and she thought they would both die, God spoke to her, showed her a well of water and rescued her. Her son, Ishmael, grew up to father a great nation.
Genesis 21.

about feelings with your children, find another adult you both trust who can take the time to talk through the children's feelings with them.

- Let your children ask you questions about the family breakdown and how it will affect them. Often they have all kinds of fears and worries, just because they've not been invited to ask questions, such as: 'Is it still all right to love both of you?' 'What will happen to me?' 'When will I be able to see daddy/mummy again?' 'Why did you break up?' 'Do you still both love me?' 'Did you break up because of me?' Answering these questions can reassure your children and help to soothe their fears.

- Many single parents find that God is a great source of comfort for them and their children. Even those who never thought they were particularly religious find that God has a new meaning for them when they try to parent on their own. Some children can also find comfort and hope from finding a faith in God, and learning how to pray, by talking to God as a friend. There are several stories in the Bible about God and Jesus helping single parent families in a special way. (See insets.)

> **Elijah was sent to the village of Zarephath during a famine. He met a widow who was gathering sticks to bake the last loaf of bread for herself and her young son. She agreed to bake the loaf for Elijah instead. From then on her flour barrel and oil jar were kept full, feeding Elijah, her son, and herself, until the end of the famine.**
> 1 Kings 17.

favour with expensive toys and treats, by giving them everything the other parent can't, or by using money to try and make up for the lost time together.

- Do all you can to help your children feel positive about themselves. Help them find their special talents and

- Be respectful of the other parent. Remember that your children need to have a healthy and positive relationship with both of their parents, as long as their safety is not at risk. It can be hard for your children to hear their parents talk disrespectfully of each other. Your children need to feel proud of both of you.

- Avoid using your children as message bearers between parents, or to 'spy' on the other parent, and then be asked to tell secrets. Try to do your own communicating with the child's other parent.

- Avoid competing with each other for your child's love, by trying to be one up on the other parent. Some parents try to buy their children's nurture them, whether it's sport, art, music, technology, being a good friend, or being a good cook. Build up your children's self-confidence and teach them life skills, such as money management, home organisation, how to fix simple things on their own, etc.

- After the emotional earthquake of a family separation the children need to feel secure again. Have a clear calendar where all family events and parental visits are clearly marked. Try to avoid last minute changes to schedules. If the children will be spending time in two parental homes, try to agree together on bedtimes, activities, homework, etc, so that the children have as few changes as possible.

> **Jesus met the funeral procession of a young man. His widowed mother wept as she followed him to his grave. Jesus knew that this mother had no one else to support her, and he raised her son from the dead and gave him back to his mother, to show his love for the widow and his concern for her situation.**
> Luke 7:11–17.

- Try to maintain contact with all the children's relatives, even the relatives of their other parent. These people are still part of their family and heritage. It may be hard at times. But try to keep an open conversation with your children about their feelings and needs.

- It's not easy being a parent on your own. There will be huge challenges, every day, every week, every wedding and funeral. No one can give you all the answers, but the greatest gift you can give your children is to encourage them to talk, and then to listen to what they have to say. Once you understand their perspective, you'll be much better equipped to help meet their needs, and to be loving enough to put their needs before your own, when necessary.

Helping victims of violence

We live in a violent world. Violence is in more places than we like to think. It's on the street corner. It's in the police station. It's in the hospital, and in the school, and it's even in our homes.

Most of us find violence unacceptable. We walk around it. Pretend it doesn't exist, keep quiet about it, and hope that it will go away, or at least, not come too close.

Violence comes in all kinds of ways. There is domestic violence in the home between husband and wife, or between parents and children. There is ethnic violence between races and tribes. Rape is physically intimate violence towards women; and there are also robberies, muggings, and physical attacks, such as stabbing, fighting and shooting. There are even attacks on elderly and disabled people.

It's not pleasant to consider violence or to be with people who have suffered violence, but we need to know how we can best support them. If we don't know how to help, then the victims of violence all around us will become the victims of our own ignorance and insensitivity. Many times, victims have been misunderstood, made to feel guilty, or hurt badly by their friends and families. Or a victim who is

looking for a safe place, some comfort, some hope, and some understanding, has been let down by a friend and that can be a greater hurt than the initial offence.

Mark – violence in the street

Mark was walking home one night. He'd been working late, and it was already dark. About halfway home he had to walk between two buildings, down a narrow path. As he reached the end of the passageway two men jumped on him, yelling and screaming. They pulled him to the ground and trod on his face. At least one of them had a knife. They took his bag and kicked him several more times before leaving him.

Mark was dazed and bleeding as he struggled to find his way home. Fortunately none of his wounds was too severe, and after a few weeks his face had healed. But Mark had other

problems. He didn't like staying late at work any more, but his family needed the money. He was afraid to walk at night, and he was afraid of narrow passageways. He was nervous as he walked down the street, afraid that someone else might attack him, or that his attackers would recognise him and treat him worse a second time. He would wake in the night after dreaming that he was being kicked, and lie there shaking with fear.

> 'There is no fear in love. But perfect love drives out fear, because fear has to do with punishment.'
> 1 John 4:18.

One night Mark's wife woke up and found him next to her, shaking with fear. She asked him what was happening and he explained about the way he'd been feeling since the attack. She listened to his feelings and his fears and held his hand as he spoke to show that she cared about him. She told him that they could manage without his extra work hours for a few weeks. She agreed to walk with him to work and back, and she asked him how she could help another time when he woke in the night. Mark said it would be helpful to him if he could hold her hand, as he just needed to know he wasn't alone.

After a few months the fears faded with the memories.

Joanne – violence in the home

Joanne had a different story. Her attack was where she least expected it, in her home. At first her husband had treated her very well, and she was very content in her marriage. But after she had her first child, her husband seemed to be jealous and suspicious about her. If she did the slightest thing wrong, he would hit her. If she stayed away from the home too long, or if the dinner didn't taste good, or his clothes had a mark on them, he would suddenly become uncontrollably angry. Once he pushed her hard up against a wall. Once he threw her to the ground. Mostly he tried to make sure that he hurt her where it wouldn't show.

Joanne didn't know what to do. She told herself it was all her fault. Ben wouldn't do these things if she were a better wife. She tried harder to make everything perfect, to cook better food, to stay at home more, and

to keep the baby quiet. But, however hard she tried, Ben still found something wrong. Often he would just be very angry with her, but he also would be physically violent.

Joanne says, 'I didn't know what to do. If I told anyone, I knew he would be even angrier, and I was afraid he'd kill me, or hurt the children. I had nowhere I could go to get away from him, and, if I left him, I thought he would just come after us and hurt us even worse.' Joanne stayed with Ben, trying to please him. She lived in fear at home, but when she went out she had to pretend everything was safe and happy.

One day, when the children saw Ben coming home they yelled out, 'Quick, Mummy, hide in here and we'll protect you from Daddy.' Joanne had accepted the violence quietly when she thought that she was the only one suffering, but when she realised that the children were growing up afraid, and feeling that they had to protect her, then she knew something had to change.

Homes need to be safe places for everyone. Every time a child sees one parent being violent towards the other, the child suffers. Often a child who sees his father being violent to his mother will one day be violent towards his own spouse. This is a cycle that needs to be broken. But it's not easy.

One day Joanne's mother came to see her just after Ben had been violent. Joanne was still sitting on the floor, dazed and shaking. A large pot lay smashed on the floor. The smallest child was clinging to her skirt and crying. Fortunately for Joanne her mother guessed her story and helped her to leave the home, with the children.

Joanne had to learn that it wasn't her fault that Ben hit her. No matter how perfect she was, he would find something to be angry about. By trying to please him all the time, hoping he would stop, and covering her wounds, she actually helped Ben to feel that he wasn't really to blame, and that what he did wasn't that serious. Joanne also realised that it wasn't fair for the children to suffer by being kept in a violent home.

Joanne's family helped her to go

away for a while to stay with a relative. No one told Ben where she was. She needed to go there to recover and feel safe. Joanne's father had a long talk with Ben, and tried to hep him admit that he had a problem. Her dad encouraged Ben to have compassion for his wife and children, and to find other ways to be angry. He helped Ben to see that he could be quite controlled with other people, and so he could also be more controlled with his wife. In everything Joanne's dad showed respect to Ben, to help him maintain his dignity.

> If we continue to turn away from the victims of violence, if we continue to hurt them with our insensitivity and thoughtless words, then we will continue to make them victims of the violence they have experienced.

Helping a victim of violence

- It's not necessary to experience violence ourselves in order to help someone through a frightening time.
- Open your mind and heart to those who have been victims.
  - Listen to their story.
  - Be there with them when they feel frightened and vulnerable.
  - Help them know that they don't have to cope alone.
  - Be a friend who will be there when they hurt and who will stay with them, whenever they need your support.
  - If they need medical, legal or financial assistance, help them to find the right people to help them.

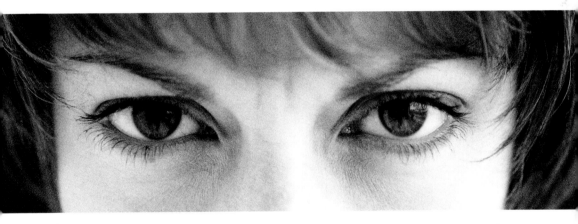

After a while, Joanne came home with the children. She was stronger and more able to cope with Ben. Ben also wanted to learn a better way. He'd been brought up in a violent home, and in his heart he didn't want his children or Joanne to suffer as he had. It wasn't going to be easy. But Joanne told him that if he ever hurt her or the children, she would leave again, and her parents offered to help support her if necessary, because they cared for her.

- Do what you can to help them feel safe.

Is there anyone you know who has been a victim of violence of any kind?
How are they coping?
Who is supporting them?
Is there anything else you could do to make their recovery easier?
Don't let them be a victim twice over.

Handling anger

The closer people are to each other, the more likely it
is that there will be times of conflict and possibly
anger. Anger can be good when it stands up for
what is right and protects the vulnerable and the
innocent. We can even be angry when we
feel that we're being made to be a victim,
and our expression of anger can help to
protect us from the person who is
abusing us.

Hot anger
Anger can be a problem when it's an
expression of our own selfishness
and in response to our own needs
not being met. When we display
anger loudly, with shouts and noise,
banging and even threatening others,
we alienate them. This kind of anger
is fiery and hot, and it's easy to see
when someone is expressing this
kind of emotion.

Cold anger
But there is another kind of anger: an
anger that's cold and quiet. It's an anger
that is silent and suppressed, that hurts us
inside and leads to resentment and
bitterness. It's often hard to see where this
anger is, but it can eat us away inside, leaving
us emotionally empty like a hollow tree.

Anger is inevitable
Feelings of anger are inevitable. At some time in
our life most of us are going to feel angry. How can
we cope with our anger in a way that won't hurt the
people around us, especially those we care for in our own
families?

Admit how you are feeling
Firstly we can admit that we feel angry. Just by saying,

'I feel really angry right now,' can help you to control some of the anger because it gives you a few moments to take some deep breaths and begin to feel calmer. Those around you also need to accept your admission of anger, not as a weakness, but as simply as if you were saying that you were thirsty, or tired.

Respect those who admit they feel angry

We need to respect those who are able to admit they're angry, and we need to avoid attacking, blaming or making them feel guilty or bad for having the feeling of anger.

Teach others how to handle you when you feel angry

It's a good idea to talk about how you can each deal with your anger at a time when you're not angry. Let each of you tell the other person how you could best be helped when you're feeling angry. One person may just need the space to walk away from the situation until feeling calmer. Another person may like to go outside and chop wood, or do some other physical work or exercise to help

> **'A gentle answer turns away wrath, but a harsh word stirs up anger.'**
> Proverbs 15:1.

use up emotional energy in a useful way, rather than being angry at people. Paul remembers his mother making bread whenever she was angry because she could bang away at the bread dough and get rid of her frustration in a safe way. Jilly wanted to be held and hugged to help her feel safe whenever she met people who were angry.

Discover the feelings hiding under the anger

When someone's angry it's important to find out what's really behind the anger. Put the anger to one side for a moment and look underneath to find different layers of emotions, such as fear, hurt, frustration, a sense of threat, rejection, disappointment, anxiety, loneliness, jealousy, helplessness, or being misunderstood or feeling victimised.

Take time to listen to the other side of the story

Sometimes when we're angry we just need to listen to the other person's story first. Then we may discover that we don't need to be angry, we really need to be caring, or helpful, or gentle.

Find ways to express your feelings positively

Be willing to share feelings. Make a list of words or pictures that describe various feelings and use them to help you express the feeling you're experiencing.

The stone bowl

One family has a bowl of different coloured stones on a small table in their home. When one of them has some strong

feelings they take out one of the coloured stones and place it on the table. If it's a blue stone, he or she feels sad. A red stone means anger, a white stone means someone feels tired and a yellow stone means that they're happy. Without talking, family members can warn each other about their feelings and the others can respond to the feelings appropriately.

Encourage positive feelings in others

Help those around you to feel good about themselves. When people feel good about themselves they are less likely to be prone to anger and to see situations as a threat.

Thinking about anger

- What happens when there is a time of anger?
- What happens before someone gets angry and what happens afterwards?

- Does each angry time follow a similar pattern?
- Are there some times when the person doesn't get angry?
- What makes the difference?
- Can you learn about how to prevent anger at other times, by noticing what happens when the person doesn't get angry?
- What would you each like to see happen when you feel angry?
- How do you think those around you can be most helpful?
- Can you change the way you see yourself or others so that you don't feel so angry?

Living with the boss!

Gary noticed that he only got angry at home. When he was at work with his boss, he wouldn't get angry about irritating and disappointing things. He would usually try to make a joke about it or be calm about the situation. But when he was at home things were different. He didn't like how angry he was, so he imagined that his boss lived in his home! When he imagined his boss being in the home, he didn't want to get angry with his family!

Keeping the family safe

Ted used to get angry with his family for not meeting his needs, until he realised that he was there to try and meet their needs, too. As a father he was there to protect his family from angry men, and that included him!

The positive perspective

Giles worked alongside a man who was always getting angry over the smallest things. Giles began to encourage the man by looking for the positive things in his work and praising him. He also told him how much he enjoyed working with him. Slowly the man began to stop getting so angry. Giles encouraged his work mate to have a sense of humour by finding new things that were funny about their work, even when things went wrong, and soon there was a better atmosphere at work.

The gentle approach

Andy was angry. He had come home early and his wife wasn't there. He expected the dinner to be ready, and that Janet would bring him a refreshing cool drink before she served the food. But she wasn't there. Where could she be? And why wasn't she there just when he needed her? A little while later she came home with their young child, Enoch. As soon as she opened the door he was yelling and screaming at her for not being there and not having his meal ready. He accused her of spending her day running after other men and gossiping in the market place. He called her 'lazy' and 'stupid'. He banged his fist on the table and told her she was a useless wife.

All through his display of anger the wife stood in the doorway holding their frightened and crying child. She was tired and she moved to sit down. He pushed her away from the chair and told her to make him a meal straight away.

Silently she made him a simple meal while the little boy clung to her legs. She served it to her husband, who was a little calmer now.

'Would you really like to know how I spent my day?' asked Janet. Andy was eating now, and so she had some space to speak. 'This morning Enoch found one of your sharp tools. I hadn't realised that you had left it on the floor. He cut his foot really badly. I had to carry him all the way to the clinic for help, wait for a long time so that he could have his foot treated, and then carry him all the way home. That's all I have done, all day. I'm going to forget that you were so angry with me. I'm going to go outside with Enoch and walk back in again and see whether you would like to respond to me in a different way.'

When others are angry with us they often expect us to respond angrily too. Surprise them by responding in a gentler way, just as Janet did with Andy, and see what a difference it can make.

How to handle stress

Overwhelmed by life

Amanda sat in the middle of her house and didn't know what to do first. There were so many clothes that needed washing that her family hardly had anything left to wear! The baby was sick, and hadn't really slept all night, and neither had she. Her husband was away for a few days, she needed to get her older children ready to go to school, and she had to do all her husband's chores too.

> 'Take my yoke upon you and learn from me, for I am gentle and humble in heart, and you will find rest for your souls.'
> Matthew 11:29.

worked with him, had fallen and broken his arm. He had no one to help him and so much work to do. Several big jobs had to be finished by the end of the week. One order was very important. If he did a good job he knew that he'd be given a much bigger order that would really help the business. But he felt that if he was behind with any of the orders, people wouldn't trust him to do the work in time in the future, and he didn't want to let anyone down. He was proud of his craftsmanship and he didn't want to cut corners to get the jobs finished, because he

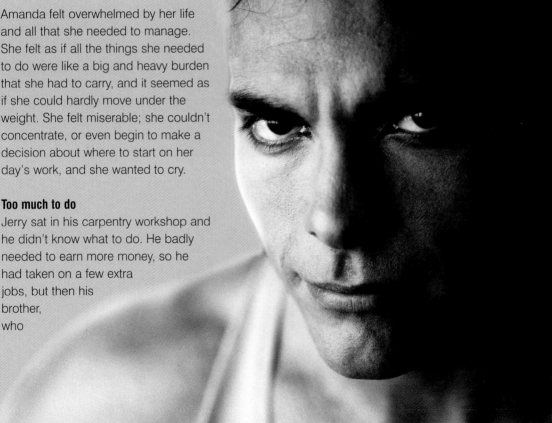

Amanda felt overwhelmed by her life and all that she needed to manage. She felt as if all the things she needed to do were like a big and heavy burden that she had to carry, and it seemed as if she could hardly move under the weight. She felt miserable; she couldn't concentrate, or even begin to make a decision about where to start on her day's work, and she wanted to cry.

Too much to do

Jerry sat in his carpentry workshop and he didn't know what to do. He badly needed to earn more money, so he had taken on a few extra jobs, but then his brother, who knew that his reputation as a carpenter depended on the quality of his work. When he tried to work, he was so anxious that he made little mistakes and he found himself getting more and more frustrated.

What is stress?

Stress is a normal part of everyday life for many people. Life is full of unavoidable stresses as well as avoidable stresses, which make our life more complicated and difficult, and prevent us from feeling happy, relaxed and confident.

Some stress is good. It can be healthy and stimulating. A little bit of stress can keep us alert and aware and can even help us to do some things better. But too much stress can be exhausting.

Often when we feel under pressure we don't relate well to those around us. We may become irritable towards our children and perhaps resentful towards our spouse, because all that we feel we have to do may seem more important at that moment than our relationships with those who are closest to us.

Stress causes tension in our bodies. We feel tight and our bodies may ache and tire more quickly. Stress seems to use up our physical and emotional energy. Difficulties seem to happen when we feel that we

aren't able to meet the demands on our energy and time, and then we start to suffer from the negative symptoms of stress.

Symptoms of stress

When a person is overstressed, it's like being ill, because they will often experience a range of symptoms.
Some of the symptoms are things like:

- Problems getting to sleep
- Problems waking up and getting started each morning

> 'Cast all your cares on the Lord and he will sustain you; he will never let the righteous fall.'
> Psalm 55:22.

- Fatigue and feeling tired all the time
- Headaches
- General pains in the body
- Feeling fidgety and finding it hard to sit still and just relax
- Unhappiness and tearfulness
- Being critical of self and others
- Lack of concentration
- Frequently forgetting things
- Problems making decisions
- Quietness and avoiding contact with other people
- Loss of self-confidence
- Feeling that life is too difficult to manage at times

Some ways to manage stress

- Stress can vary from person to person. What will be very stressful for one will be exciting and interesting for another person. We're all different and what makes us stressed will be different too, as well as the ways in which we respond to stress. When we realise that someone is stressed it's important not to expect him to behave the same way we would in the situation. One person may find it stressful being alone and struggling all by himself. Another person might find it stressful if there are too many people around. One person may respond to stress by being quiet and withdrawn, while another person may respond by being noisy and cross with everyone.
- Some of the biggest causes of avoidable stress are expectations. It may be that we feel other people expect too much of us. Or it may be that we expect too much of ourselves. Expectations can be good. They give us goals to aim for, but when we don't reach up to the expectations of others, and ourselves, we can feel as if we've failed. When we manage everything perfectly, it seems that nobody notices how well we are coping. It's only when we don't live up to their expectations that people begin to grumble and complain about us.
- We can't take all of the stress out of our lives. Unexpected things happen. There are natural disasters, babies get sick, people make mistakes from time to time, and have accidents. But there are some things we can do to minimise the extra and avoidable stresses in our lives.
- We can try to set realistic goals for ourselves. If we set out to do three things in a day, and we only ever manage to complete one of those things, maybe we need to set ourselves only one goal for the day, and then feel good when we've completed

that. If we're putting the pressure on ourselves because our expectations are too high, we need to lower the expectations we have of ourselves. It's better to do one thing at a time and feel good about what we've done, than to try and do too much and feel bad because we can't do everything.

- Balance work with pleasure. Don't work all the time. After doing a particularly difficult task, reward yourself with something you enjoy doing, and have a break.
- Get plenty of sleep. When we feel rested we are much more able to cope with the stresses of the day. If you're a mum, try to nap when your baby does, or find someone to help you with the children so you can have your own rest.
- Find some help. Challenging jobs are always easier and more enjoyable when the work is shared with a friend.
- Plan ahead if you think there'll be a challenge coming. Do one small part of the job at a time, and spread the load over several days or weeks. Find extra people who can support you and help you through challenging times, such as a friend or family member you feel comfortable with. Don't try to do as much as

you normally do when you feel under pressure.

- Learn to say 'no'. Sometimes we suffer stress because we find it hard to say 'no' to people who ask us for help. Whenever we say 'yes' to others we are saying 'no' to our own family.
- Find out what helps you to feel better. Some people find hugs relaxing. Others like to go for a walk on their own. Amanda found it helped when she took ten minutes a day to work on a sewing project, and Jerry liked to do some heavy sawing when he felt stressed. Think of a few things you enjoy doing that help you to feel more relaxed, and choose one to do each time you sense that you're getting more stressed. Find time to laugh, because a good laugh always relaxes the body, or do something energetic to use up the extra stress energy in your body.
- Remind yourself that you don't need to know everything, and you don't need to do everything perfectly. It's all right not to be perfect, and it's all right to make mistakes.
- If something you do seems to make you feel stressed, ask yourself, 'What am I doing this for? Am I trying to show someone how good I am? Is it making me a better person, or is it making me into a miserable person? When I do this, what effect does it have on those I love? Are they happier or sadder because of what I'm doing? What would they want me to do if they could choose?'

What can you do today to take some of the stress out of your life, or out of someone else's life? You can spread stress and anxiety, or peace and joy. What will you choose?

Preparing for retirement

Retirement may seem a long way off when you have a young family, but it's good to start preparing for it as soon as you can. You may also have aging family members who need to begin thinking about their retirement plans.

Taking care of your marriage

For most couples retirement will be unlike the life they have known when one or both of them were working. It could be the first time in their lives that they are both at home together, and they need to think about how they will manage this new phase of their life. Some couples enjoy the time getting to know each other again, and often manage better when they each have specific times to pursue their interests separately. Others might like to meet up with groups of friends. Some may need to have another look at how they distribute the household tasks of cooking, cleaning, gardening, shopping, etc, so that one person doesn't feel as if she is doing all the work.

It may be useful to have a look at the 'Marriage' chapters of this book to find ways of building closeness as you both grow older.

Wider family

You might want to think about your position in your wider family. Are there family members who need a little extra help because they have young children, a heavy work-load, or an illness? How might you be able to make their lives a little easier? If you have a large family, where you see lots of needs, how will you share your time among them?

> 'Grey hair is a crown of splendour; it is attained by a righteous life.'
> Proverbs 16:31.

Finances

Plan your finances as early as you can in life. As the financial climate is always changing, get the best advice available. It's also a good idea to have a variety of investments to help you save for your pension and retirement. In some cases, younger family members help to take care of the older members. But whatever you think will happen, it is good to plan ahead and have several options. It is also important to make a wise will, considering the effect of your will on your whole family, and the possibility of showing love and grace through how you choose to share out your goods after your death.

- How close are shops and services like doctors and hospitals?
- What else would you like to have nearby?
- What if you could no longer drive, or walk far, how easy would it be to live in the chosen place?
- Can you follow your interests and hobbies easily?

Housing

It is a good idea to think about your housing as you retire. Pat and Keith loved gardening and chose a house with a huge garden for their retirement. For a couple of years they enjoyed working together in the garden,

Places to live

- It is useful to think carefully about where you would like to live.
- Consider who else lives nearby.
- How near are your family members and/or friends if they need to come and see you or help you?
- Where is the closest church?

> **'Rise in the presence of the aged, show respect for the elderly, and revere your God. I am the Lord.'**
> Leviticus 19:32

planting vegetables and flowers. But then Keith had a stroke and was paralysed down one side, He had to use a wheelchair and couldn't manage the garden. Pat had to look after Keith and it was sad for them to watch their lovely garden become overgrown once more. They wished they had chosen a home with a smaller garden, and then rented an allotment garden. Their two-storey home also became difficult to manage as it was hard for Keith to get upstairs. Unless you like to move during your retirement, it is often better to choose a small manageable home on one level, with flat entrances, as you will be more likely to find this adaptable to your needs if you become less mobile.

Hobbies and Interests

Perhaps you might like to develop the hobbies and interests you already have. Maybe you need some

Lord, You know better than I know myself that I am growing older. Keep me from getting too talkative, and thinking I must say something on every subject and on every occasion. Release me from craving to straighten out everybody's affairs. Teach me the glorious lesson that occasionally it is possible that I may be mistaken. Make me thoughtful, but not moody; helpful, but not bossy; for you know, Lord, that I want a few friends at the end.

Anonymous.

activities you can do on your own, and some that you can enjoy together with your spouse or friends. Hobbies can give you lots of opportunities that you may miss once you have stopped work, such as an opportunity to meet friends, to attend regular events, to have a sense of achievement, and even to provide extra income possibilities.

Using your work skills

Maybe you could use some of your work skills to help others. Some retirees train and mentor young people, or apprentices. Some volunteer their skills for community development projects in their own area, or even in another country. The skills and knowledge you have developed over the years are very valuable resources to pass on to others, and you might like to think how you could do this.

Staying safe

Health and safety are important issues throughout our lives, but as we grow older we need to take extra care of ourselves. A healthy diet with lots of fruit and vegetables, and plenty of water, helps to maintain a strong body. Older people also need to protect their bodies from too much heat or cold, and are also at greater risk of falling and hurting themselves badly. Getting up slowly, wearing supportive foot-wear, and having safe floor surfaces without slippery rugs that can slide or trip, can all help to prevent falls. Also consider the danger of small animals that run around your feet, and make sure that all your furniture is stable and secure, in case you hold onto it for support. It can be a good idea to sort through your things and decide what you want to keep and what you no longer need, so that your home is less cluttered, and easier to keep tidy.

Reflecting on your life

Take an appreciative look at your life, and think about the happy memories, the accomplishments, the things you felt really good about. Think about the differences you made in the world, even in the smallest ways, by being a good friend, planting some flowers, or by encouraging a child. Think about the contribution you could still make in the future. Think of the stories and skills you would like to pass on to your grandchildren, or other people.

Health

Think about your exercise and diet and consider whether you need to make some changes as you grow older. It's good to do at least some gentle exercise each day and to eat plenty of fruit and vegetables. You may like to ask

your doctor about any ideas he has about how you could keep yourself healthy, considering your medical and health history. Do you need glasses, stronger lenses, or a hearing aid?

Church and Mission

Retirement can be a special opportunity for serving God in new and exciting ways. Ask God to show you where he would like you to work, and how you can use your gifts and skills in an area of ministry that you find rewarding. Maybe this will be in your local church, or in your community, or even in another country. Finding a ministry activity that you can share with your spouse, or other family members, and that blends your skills and interests, can be a positive way to build closeness as you work together.

Retirement may be the end of one way of living and working, but it is also the beginning of a new way of living and working, that can be a time for focusing on fulfilling relationships and activities.

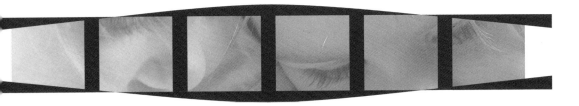

Chapter 6

Reaching out to other relationships

How to be a 'great' grandparent!

Being a grandparent is a special experience. It's a time to enjoy another generation, to be a good role model, and to relive some of your own childhood. Anyone can be a grandparent, but it takes someone special to be a 'great grand-parent'!

Here are some ideas collected from seasoned 'great' grandparents!

- Remember that many childcare practices have changed in the last thirty years, and let the new parents guide you through the maze of current ideas! Whatever you do, avoid making them feel guilty for not doing things the way you did – let them find their own way. They'll usually ask for your help and advice when they're most ready for it.
- Time is more important than money to your grandchildren. They enjoy someone who has the time to play football with them, read to them, tell them stories, and teach them new skills.
- Children often need someone who will spend time really listening to them. The best way to listen is to hear what the child has to say, without judging the child. Listen to his feelings and feel with him. Show you understand. Tell stories of how you managed when you were in a similar situation.
- Find ways to laugh with your grandchildren! Tell them jokes on the phone, email them pages of funny stories,

send them cartoons that you know will really appeal to them. When you're with them, laugh, make a fool of yourself, and let your grandchildren play some safe practical jokes on you. Children love adults who'll enter their world and enjoy their sense of humour.

- Make something together with your grandchildren, a tree house, an animal cage, a loaf of bread, a garden. This will give your grandchildren special memorirs of time spent with you, and they'll feel proud of what you made together.

- If you live a long way from your grandchildren you could write them encouraging letters, or send cheerful postcards. Children love to get something in the post. You can also find things your grandchildren enjoy, or topics in which they are interested, and look out for tiny books, or articles in magazines, to send to them.

- Keep your promises to your grandchildren. Let them know they can trust you. In an uncertain world, knowing that your family can always be depended on is a great feeling!

- Tell your life story to your grandchildren, or even make a small book of stories if you can.

- Create traditions together with your grandchildren, special places you visit annually, special food you always make when they come, etc. One grandma arranges the food on her grandchildren's plates so that it makes simple pictures. One meal the food will be

arranged like a face, or a tree, a flower, or a butterfly. It's simple to do, but it brings a smile to the children's faces every time!

- Avoid criticising your grandchildren; find something positive to say instead. Criticism may push them away from you.

- If a grandchild says or does something inappropriate, which needs correction, do so, but in a fun way. You could say, 'I'll pretend I didn't hear that! Would you like another chance?!'

'Children's children are a crown to the aged.'
Proverbs 17:6.

- Discipline them lovingly. It's important to handle discipline in a careful and positive way that doesn't undermine their own parents' wishes, or criticise their parents in any way.
- Above all, encourage your grandchildren to aim high and be the best they can be. Give them all the tools, encouragement and guidance necessary. Believe in them, and accept them, no matter what they do. Show them unconditional love.
- Make your home a safe place where they can find love and comfort during the difficult times, and you'll be like their island in a stormy world. If your grandchild's home has been broken by any kind of event or tragedy, you need to be more supportive and wiser than ever.
  - Pray for your grandchildren. Share your faith with them, but also be respectful of their own family's faith ideas.
  - Children are the future generation. They will be happier, stronger, more talented and more secure when we give them a stable, enjoyable and encouraging foundation.

Someone said. 'If you really want to be significant, love a child.' A hundred years from now it may not matter what you did, or how big your house was, or how much money you had. But what will matter is the difference you made in the life of a child.

Creating a welcoming home

A welcoming home is a wonderful gift. A home doesn't need to be big, or even beautiful, to be welcoming. You can visit the most wonderful building in the world and still not feel welcome and at ease, because it's too perfect. If you sit down you feel you might ruffle the cushions, and you're afraid you might break something. But it's lovely to enter a home that's relaxing and refreshing, where you feel you can be yourself.

Hospitality at home

- Whenever you offer hospitality, pray, and ask God to match what you offer with the needs of your guest.
- One of the secrets of creating a welcoming home is to think of other people's needs first. What do your visitors need most? Is it a drink, some food, a place to sit and rest, or maybe even some sleep? Or is it a place where someone will look after them for a few moments, and where they can rest from all their burdens and responsibilities?
- It doesn't matter how simple our home, we can usually offer guests a place to sit down and rest, some shade from the sun, or some warmth, if it is cold. We can usually offer them a drink and share whatever food we have with them.
- Even the simplest and smallest home, a tent, a few pieces of old metal, a home made out of mud bricks, can be a welcoming place when it's neat and tidy and the floor is clean and swept. A table can look lovely laid with fresh leaves and flowers, or even with a simple arrangement of smooth stones, or a piece of colourful fabric. Use the things you have already, and a few things you have

found in nature, to make your home attractive and unique.

- Each culture has its own special ways to welcome others. Some welcome with a garland of flowers, some with an elaborate feast, some with rituals. These can be lovely, but most of all people often want a place where they can relax. Your guests may never remember what they ate, or how perfect your home was, but they'll usually remember the atmosphere, and whether they felt comfortable and at ease, or whether they felt awkward and out of place.

- One of the important aspects of being welcoming is to be prepared. Know exactly what you'll do if you invite someone into your home, what food you'll serve, what dishes you'll use, and what role each person will have.

- It's also important to discuss hospitality as

> 'Do not forget to entertain strangers, for by so doing some people have entertained angels without knowing it.'
> Hebrews 13:2.

a family to check that everyone has an understanding of what being welcoming means. It's helpful if possible invitations are discussed as a family before an event, to check that everyone's prepared for the occasion. It's not easy for a wife if her husband brings people home without asking her first! It's polite and respectful to check with each other first! But there will always be times when people need a welcoming place in an emergency.

Who needs welcoming?

- Often it's our wider family whom we welcome into our home for family celebrations, during family emergencies, and just to strengthen family bonds.

- Then there are the people who are our friends, who come over to spend time with us, to share in a special occasion, or to help them out during a difficult time.

- Around us there are people we know, but not very well. Some of them may be lonely, or struggling. Some of them may be unhappy, or ill, or disabled. Some may be tired, or be poorer than you. This is where a welcoming home can do something wonderful.
- Look out for the people on the edges of your lives who need a few moments of peace and beauty, away from the worries of their struggles. Let them have the comfort and hope of knowing that somebody cares for them and has noticed their need for a welcoming home.
- Or take your welcoming heart to their own home, bringing them a hot meal and taking some time to do some of the jobs that they're finding it hard to do on their own.
- There are also the strangers who are passing through our lives who may need to share in our love and care for a while.
- Even though there are many people who need some hospitality, the most important people to be welcoming towards are your own children and your spouse.

> **'Share with God's people who are in need. Practise hospitality.'**
> Romans 12:13.

- Consider how you can each show hospitality to the other members in the family, and extend your graciousness to your own children.

Think about it

- Who needs welcoming into your home?
- How does it feel if you are a child in a family which is always so busy welcoming others that you feel that your parents don't have time to be welcoming to you?
- If the mother is usually the one helping to create a welcoming atmosphere in the home, how can the rest of the family show *her* some hospitality from time to time?

Hospitality for mum

In the Jones' family, whenever mum looks tired, one of the children will offer to make her favourite drink. Each of the children, even the smallest one, knows how to make mum's drink just the way she likes it. The other children will encourage mum to find a

comfortable place to sit down, and insist that she stay there until she's finished the drink. While she sips the drink slowly, the children quietly tidy the room, or begin to make a meal.

Hospitality towards children

Harry and Fiona did something that was very unusual in their culture. Once a week both parents would serve a meal to the children to show them hospitality and honour. Occasionally the children would serve the parents instead, and by so doing the parents taught the children good welcoming skills. Whenever visitors came by, the children were confident in offering hospitality too, because the skills had been modelled and learned so well in their family.

Hospitality towards children's friends

Katy and Jim
Stewart liked
to know

that their children were safe, and felt much happier when their children were close to the family home. The parents encouraged the children to bring their own friends into the family home. There was a shelf with cups, a jug of cool water, and some little things to eat so that the children could welcome their friends whenever they wanted to, and serve them any items that were on the 'welcome shelf'.

Being a hospitable guest

Whenever Sam was invited to share a meal with someone he would always take a small gift. He liked to show some hospitality to his hosts by giving them a pot or a basket that he'd made, or he would see something that needed doing in the home, and offer to fix it for them.

Whenever we share what we have with others, it seems as if we gain more than we give. Who can you welcome into your home today?

How to be a good friend

Friends are important to us. Without friends we would feel so alone and unsupported. Friends bring happiness into our lives. Think for a moment about your friends and how your life would be without them.

Someone once said, 'In order to *have* a good friend, you need to *be* a good friend.' By being a good friend to others, we'll often find we have good friends just when we need them the most.

'A friend loves at all times.'
Proverbs 17:17.

So what can we do to make sure that we're the best friends we can be to those around us?

Friends can listen to each other

Listening to someone is like giving a gift. Many people know how to talk, but few know how to really listen. It's by listening to each other that we're able to know each other better. When we listen we can identify the other's feelings, and then respond to them. We can discover their dreams and help to make them come true. And we can find out what their needs are, so that we know how to meet those needs in the best way possible.

Friends accept each other

Friends are people who know all about you and still love you! That's an amazing thought! None of us is perfect, we all make mistakes and have our peculiar little habits, but a real friend will accept everything that

we are, and continue to love us. We can return that by loving them just the way they are, and not expecting them to be perfect either.

Friends know how to forgive

Even friends may hurt each other at times, but they know how to forgive each other, knowing that they may also need to be forgiven in the future. Friends treat each other the way they'd most like to be treated.

Friends believe the best in each other

Someone once described this like a man holding some grains in his hand. He rubs his hands to loosen the chaff around the grain, and then gently blows away the unwanted husks forever, and keeps the grain. Friends hold on to the best understanding they have of us and throw away the bits that aren't useful, letting

the imperfect memories of the other person blow away forever in the breeze of forgiveness and love.

Friends share in each other's emotions

When one friend is happy, the other is happy for them, without being jealous. When one friend is sad, the other is sad with them, and comforts them by sharing in their grief. Frances sat with Mary and shared her sorrow when she had a miscarriage. She didn't try to cheer her up, or tell her she'd have another baby one day, or even tell her not to cry over a miscarriage. Frances just sat and was sad with her, even shedding her own tears.

Friends help each other practically

Good friends are willing to share and be helpful wherever they can to make life easier for those around them. Friends will do amazing things for each other. A friend will walk two miles with you when you only asked him to walk one. A friend will lend you not only a pair of trousers if you need them, but also a matching shirt! Friends share their special talents to help each other. John will mend Mark's roof, while Mark helps John's son with his schoolwork.

Friends anticipate each other's needs and meet them quietly.

Molly had been ill, and she had really appreciated it when her mother had sent over meals every day for her family, so that she didn't have to cook. When her friend Janine was sick, Molly thought she might appreciate some meals too, especially as Janine's mother had died the year before.

Friends make sacrifices for each other

Martin's son was very sick. He needed to take him to the doctor, who was ten miles away, but he had no car, and his son was in pain. It would be difficult to carry his son all that way, but Martin had no other way to get him to the doctor. Martin's friend, David had a truck that he needed to use for work. If he let Martin use the truck, then he would lose a day's work, but David could see that Martin's need was great. David drove Martin and his son to the doctor's, waited while the boy was treated and then drove them back home again. Martin appreciated the sacrifice that Martin made for him, and decided that he wanted to find a way to do the same for David one day.

Friends delight each other

They surprise each other and enrich each other's lives. Friends look for different and exciting ways to celebrate their friendships. Hannah had always admired a beautiful dress

that Queenie wore. Queenie had made it herself, but she'd taken the time to decorate it by sewing patterns of flowers around the hem. One day Hannah found a package waiting for her in her home. When she opened it she found a dress just like Queenie's, but in Hannah's favourite colours.

Treasure your friends

Friends are a wonderful way to make our lives happier and more interesting and meaningful. We can treasure the friends we have and let them know how happy we are to have them as our friends. We can also take the time to make new friends. Look out for people who may need your friendship, people who may not be able to return your help or hospitality, such as poor people, sick people, strangers in your community, people who seem to be sad and lonely for different reasons.

Everybody needs friends

What kind of friend will you be? The more you give to others, of time, and help and understanding, the more will come back to you, often just when you need it most.

Living happily with the generations

Communities always seem to be stronger and more successful when people live close to their wider families. When generations of a large family live close together they can offer practical support, help and wisdom to each other. Older people have wisdom and stories to share, younger people can help support the older generations, everyone can come together in a crisis, or in a celebration, or to build a new home.

How we live with our families will vary from place to place. In some countries the younger generations often have to move away from their multi-generational families in order to study and find work and safety for their families. They often feel isolated and have the challenge of trying to live without the support of parents, grandparents, aunts, uncles and cousins, but they may have the advantage of being able to make a new start as a family, away from the pressures of other family members.

Other families will stay closely together, and have the challenge of being close, but not too close, so that there is an acceptance of new family members.

A healthy family will also be open to new possibilities, and doesn't insist on everything being done the same way all the time.

One of the important features of a successful and happy family is a respect for every person, young and old, male and female, even though the way respect is shown will differ depending on the age and experience of the person.

Building good relationships with the older generation

- When a new family is formed through the marriage of a man and a woman, two families reach out and join hands. This is not always an easy union. The couple themselves will be adjusting to a new life and their families need to adjust to their new position. The husband and wife need to know that both their families are respected, even if one family is poorer or less educated, or has a different status.
- It's important for husbands and wives to discuss how they will respond to their own families when they wish to be involved in their lives. They need to agree together about how involved they feel their families can be, as this will vary from couple to couple. How will the husband respond if his parents start criticising his wife, or telling the couple what to do? How will the wife respond if her family isn't happy with her husband, or make too many demands on her?
- Communication is an important key to happy intergenerational families. Let your parents know what your plans are. Agree together the boundaries your new family needs within the wider boundary of the larger family.
- Don't be afraid to ask advice from the older generation when they have more knowledge and experience. This makes them feel honoured and respected.
- Accept practical support from your parents whenever they offer to help. You may need to be clear about the help you need, but, when you have a young family, life can be very tiring. One of the greatest gifts that your parents can offer is caring for the young children sometimes so that the mother can rest or do other tasks.

- If your family offers you financial support, think about what it will mean, and handle this very sensitively. Will the husband's family be offended if the wife's family helps financially? Does the money come with conditions that you must do this or that, or live here, or work there? If so, are you happy with the agreement? Will other siblings be jealous of the money you may receive? What might happen in the future if you do or do not accept the money?
- Be aware of the dangers and resentment that can build up if one of you is too involved with your own parents.
- Try to deal with issues as they arise – don't let them fester into misunderstandings and feuds.
- One useful tip is to consider ten things that you appreciate about your spouse's

parents and families. Then to think of how these attributes can be used to strengthen the family. Then, when parents want to help, you will know the best way to use their skills without causing any resentment.

- Whenever the parents respond helpfully, sensitively and discreetly, let them know that you appreciate the way they've responded, and give clear information about what you've found especially helpful.

- When your families become too involved in your life, politely and firmly let them know that you appreciate that they're trying to be helpful, but that there are some things that you need to deal with on your own as a couple.

Building good relationships with the younger generation

- What if you're one of the older generations? Welcoming newcomers into your family by marriage can be a challenge. Whoever they are they will have been brought up in a family other than yours. Even if you've lived together in the same small village, families have different ways of doing things.

- Be sensitive to the needs of the new family members. They will make mistakes, and they won't be perfect, just as you weren't when you were young. Look for the positive qualities in the newcomer to your family and think about them.

- Will and Hannah were concerned about their son's new wife. She wasn't as quietly spoken as their daughters and she had new ways of preparing the food. Whenever Hannah was with Alice she would notice all the things she did wrong and then go and tell her son. She tried to get Paul to talk to Alice and make her change, but Paul wouldn't. Paul told his mother that Alice was just perfect for him and he liked the way she chatted to him and the food she made for him. Paul protected Alice from his mother's criticism and slowly Hannah began to accept Alice.

- Be helpful to the new family when you can be, without interfering, and let them develop their own relationship, and their own way of being together, which may be different from your way. It's often better to say nothing than to risk offending somebody and causing a family feud.

- Let the younger ones come and ask you for your wisdom when they need it, as usually they'll appreciate it more when they ask for it, than when you think they may need to hear it. It can be very hard, but be prepared that the couple may not always follow your advice. Sometimes they have difficult decisions to make in a world that's new and changing, very unlike the world you knew a generation ago.

- Try not to take sides in a family disagreement. Especially avoid siding with the wife, or the husband. You'll all have to live together after the problem has long been solved, and so avoid doing anything that may damage a relationship and make it hard to live together happily in the future.
- Alex and Annie had five children. Some of them weren't doing everything they would have liked, but they were all their children and they loved them. Each year they gave each child the same amount of money to use as he or she wished, so that there would be no jealousy and resentment.
- Whatever happens, wise parents and grandparents keep accepting the younger generations, in spite of their mistakes and disagreements. Even when they make poor choices and have to suffer the results of their decisions, be there to support and love them. Families are important and everyone needs each other. One day you'll need the young ones too.

Thinking about it

- Are there some bonds in your family that need strengthening?
- Does your son have a wife who needs to know you love and accept her?
- Do you have a grandchild who needs forgiving?
- Do you need to forgive a parent for offending your wife?

Whenever you're not sure what to do to strengthen your family, love, acceptance and forgiveness are often good guidelines. Be wise, handle your family with love, give them the space to grow in their own direction, and be there for them whatever sorrows come their way.

Relating to someone with a disability

Mike's story

As soon as Mike was born, it was obvious life wasn't going to be easy for him. He was born without a right foot, and his right hand was deformed, with just a thumb and two short fingers. In the community where he was born it was customary for babies with disabilities to be left to die. It was a poor village and the families didn't have the resources to care for a child who would face physical challenges and not be able to hunt and farm to create food.

But Mike's father had waited years for a son. He saw the disabilities, but he also saw the possibilities. He and his wife nurtured their young son, giving him good food to help him be strong. When the boy started to creep around, his father made him a little wheeled chair to sit in and he could use his left foot to help move the chair and steer it.

His father even bandaged his own right hand, until it worked like Mike's deformed hand, so that he could learn how to help Mike use his hands. When Mike began to walk, his father carved a crutch for him, to help him get around and one day he had an idea for making a wooden foot for Mike's leg. Soon there wasn't much that Mike couldn't do by himself.

Mike grew to be wise and kind. He and his father would invent new things to help him get around and do different tasks. They began to make things for the other people in their community who were sick and disabled. Mike would go and listen to their stories and their hopes, and he and his father would try to help each one of them to find a useful job to do for the community.

Because of Mike's wisdom, kindness and understanding, he grew up to be a good leader in his community.

Here are some of the things that Mike's community learned from this experience

This could happen to any one of us

It's sad when someone is born with an obvious disability, but most of us have something in our lives that stops us from achieving everything we could. Any of us could become disabled during our lives, through illness or an accident. If that happened, we would want people to treat us with respect, listen to us and help us when necessary. It's useful to think how we would like to be treated if we had a disability, and to use our thoughts to guide us in the way we treat others with a disability. When Mike explained to people what his life was like, they realised that more needed to be done to help the other disabled people in their community.

Value everyone

It's important to value others, and to treasure them, even when they are not physically perfect. They are still important human beings who can participate in our communities. Even those who seem to be so disabled that they can't even move can be an asset in their community. The measure of a strong and caring community is often seen in the way it treats those who need the most support and help.

Listen to them

We can listen to their perspective on our world as they often have valuable insights from their experiences. Someone who is deaf, blind, can't walk, or who is disfigured, may be able to help us see better ways of relating to each other, or new ways to do things.

Help them to make a contribution to the community

We can help people with a disability find something that they can contribute to the community. People need to be able to feel that they can do something useful. Beethoven, one of the great European composers, was totally deaf when he wrote some of his most wonderful pieces of music. Stephen Hawking is a famous British scientist and author, even though he is totally paralysed. Someone who can't walk can write, draw, weave, make pots, or even be a teacher! Blind people can often make things with their hands, listen to people, tell stories to children, or play wonderful music.

Help them to conquer their environment

Often the biggest challenge for people with disabilities is their environment. Help them to overcome environmental barriers by finding ways they can move around safely, reach the things they need, and take care of their own personal needs. It may be that you have to think up new ways to make their clothes, new places to put things, or unusual ways of doing things. Mike's village worked hard to make a smooth pathway for his chair with wheels on it, so that he was free to move around safely and easily.

Treat them with respect

Treat everyone with a disability or illness with respect, as any other human being with feelings and needs. To treat them with any less respect than you would like to be treated yourself can give them emotional and social disabilities that can be even more difficult to cope with than their original disability. Ask them how they would like to be helped by you, what they want from life, and what they'd like to contribute to the community, and then try to put their ideas into action.

Help them to find the best medical help

If people need medical help, help them to find it. Little Luke was badly disfigured because he had a cleft palate, and even some of his nose was missing. His mother had rejected him at birth and her parents had taken the child into their home to care for him. One day his grandfather heard that there were some doctors visiting the big city who could mend faces. He carried little Luke for miles to the big city to find the doctors. It was a difficult job, but after many hours of work they were able to make a new face for little Luke. For days his face was covered in bandages, and full of stitches, but when Luke's new face was revealed, his grandfather cried for joy! Luke would now be like any other child! Back home, his mother accepted him once more and Luke's life was transformed.

Help them to get a good education

Try to help a disabled child to have as good an education as possible. This may take some creativity, depending on the child's disability. Perhaps a special desk or chair needs to be made, or perhaps a blind child needs another child he can trust to write down his answers, or to read to him. Pictures and words can help deaf children to learn. Whatever they can learn will help them in the

future. Many disabled people can do all kinds of jobs with some education and training, a little thoughtfulness, and some adaptations.

Plan for their needs

When planning community events, or a public building project, make sure that the needs of the disabled users are taken into consideration. Can they get into the building? How will they experience what is happening? Can they use the toilet facilities? What would make the event more comfortable for the disabled person, or the building more useful? Make sure that the voices of the disabled people are heard and that their opinions and ideas are listened to and considered to be valid and useful.

Support their family in caring for them

Find ways to help the family of a disabled person if they are carrying a large burden of caring for a sick or disabled person. Perhaps you could help with some of the care, or do simple things like making a meal for the

family, or doing some laundry, or helping with some other practical tasks that the family would find difficult. When Joseph was blinded after a short illness, his brothers decided to help his family by doing some of the heavy jobs around the home. They mended his roof and chopped his firewood until Joseph's sons were big enough to take care of the jobs on their own.

The whole community benefits

Some communities are already very good about involving people of all abilities; others still have a long way to go. But those who have taken the time to listen to, and learn from disabled people, have found that the whole community can benefit when the needs of the disabled person are considered.

When you help make this world a better place for someone with a disability, you help to make it a better place for everyone. And one day you may find yourself in need of that better place.

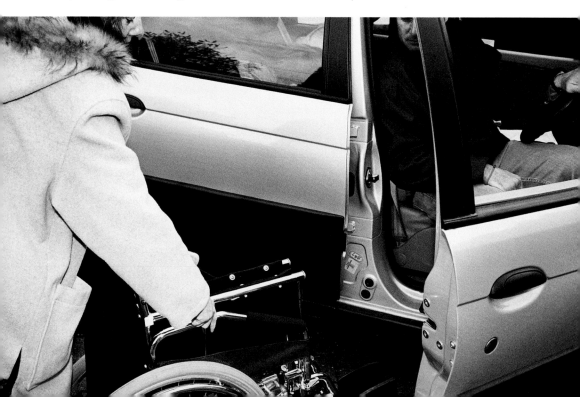

Encouraging your pastor and his family

An important aspect of Christian service is encouraging our church leaders. These ideas can be adapted to involve the whole family in showing love and support for your local church leaders and teachers.

'Now we ask you, brothers, to respect those who work hard among you, who are over you in the Lord and who admonish you. Hold them in the highest regard in love because of their work.'
1 Thessalonians 5:12, 13.

- Find something positive to say to the pastor each week.
- Pray for the family, and ask them for their specific prayer requests.
- Invite the pastor and his family for a meal. Usually they are the ones providing the hospitality; give them some in return!
- Treat them to tickets for a special day out on their own.
- Offer free babysitting so they can go out together on their own, or attend a special church event together.
- Ask for specific ways in which you can help, and then do what you have promised to do, as well as you can.
- Ask the pastor's wife for the list of all the jobs on the home 'to-do' list, and then arrange for competent members to offer to help do the odd jobs, gardening, etc. Often the pastor is so busy helping others that he doesn't have much time to work on his own home and garden.
- Bake a cake or dessert for the family. Take the time to find their favourite foods, especially things the children will like.
- Plan a surprise party to honour them.
- Pay for the couple to have a weekend away together, perhaps at a Christian marriage retreat, etc.

- Give the pastor's wife a bouquet of the church flowers after the service.
- Give them some book vouchers; pastors are always buying books!
- Find out if the pastor has a hobby, and buy him something to match the hobby, such as special tools, garden plants, art materials, music, new guitar strings, etc. Do this for the wife as well.
- Guard their days off, and family meal times, and avoid calling them at these times, or too late at night.
- Try to attend as many church events as practical, to show your support for all aspects of the church. If you can't go, be considerate and send your apologies.
- Find fun ways to show your friendship to the pastor and his wife. Most people are serious with them, and they need to have some fun and happy relationships. Find out what makes them smile and think of ways to make their life brighter!

Bringing it all together

It can be helpful to read a book like this and get some fresh ideas for your family, but you probably have lots of your own family wisdom that you have gathered throughout your life.

Try this exercise to help you appreciate some of the things you and your family have learned along the way, things that will help you as you plan for the future of your family.

Family Network Plan

- Make a diagram of your family, a family tree, showing at least three generations, or as much as you can manage.

- Lay the pieces out on a big piece of paper and move them around until they are in the right places.
- Start with yourself and your brothers and sisters at the bottom of the diagram, then your parents and their families, and your grandparents and their families above them.
- Use stones, buttons, or circles of paper with names written on to represent people.
- It's helpful if you use different colours to show who is male and who is female.
- If there are other people who were (or are) important to your family, include them as well.
- Consider the stories you know about

these people, and next to each name write the things you think they did right, and the lessons you can learn from their family experiences.

Think about your current family:
- What wisdom have you gathered from your family heritage to help you with your own family?
- What hopes do you have for your family?
- What are you doing to make those hopes become a reality?
- What strengths does each person have in your family?
- What help and resources do you have to support you as you live together as a family?
- What other help would you like?

- Where might you be able to get the help you need?
- How do you think our all-loving God sees your family?
- What do you think God would most like to do for family members to show how much he loves them?
- How can you help God to show this love to your family members, remembering that we have been given the special job of helping each other to experience the amazing, accepting and grace-filled love of God?
- Spend some time thanking God for the people in your family, praying for their special needs and asking how God would like to work with you to demonstrate his love for them.

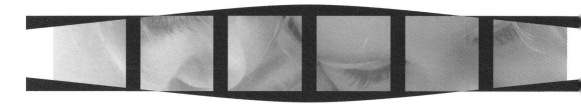

Chapter 7

AIDS and the family

by **Richard Willis** MA MSc FRSH FRIPHH AITV MIPHE

Family danger

Families suffer when even one person in the family suffers. Often we bring suffering upon ourselves through the things that we say or do (either ignorantly or wilfully), thus bringing danger to the stability of the family circle, a danger that is far more widespread than we might think.

As the Director-General of the World Health Organisation, Dr Gro Harlem Bruntland puts it: 'The world is living dangerously – either because it has little choice, or because it is making the wrong choices.'

Nowhere are these choices so far-reaching as those which concern our sexual behaviour and in situations where there is a risk of contracting sexually-transmitted diseases (STDs). Down through the years these diseases have damaged families through the disablement, disfigurement, separation and isolation of family members.

Global summary of the HIV/AIDS epidemic 2002

Number of people living with HIV/AIDS	Total	42 million
	Adults	38.6 million
	Women	19.2 million
	Children under 15 years	3.2 million
People newly infected with HIV in 2002	Total	5 million
	Adults	4.2 million
	Women	2 million
	Children under 15 years	800,000
AIDS deaths in 2002	Total	3.1 million
	Adults	2.5 million
	Women	1.2 million
	Children under 15 years	610,000

UNAIDS/WHO

For example, in the past, before modern treatment options, syphilis affected not only the person incubating the disease but also his/her offspring congenitally. Untreated, many of the people in whom the syphilis had run through to its final (or tertiary) stage ended up institutionalised with general paralysis of the insane (GPI). The stigma of having someone in the family with syphilis led to denial on the part of the family, the break-up of families, and the locking-up and neglect of the family member.

The latest of the STDs, and having an even more devastating effect on the family, is HIV/AIDS. Adults and children have been affected not only physically but emotionally and socially as this particular STD has run its course. A UNICEF • UNAIDS • WHO Report says: 'Today's youth have inherited a lethal legacy that is killing them and their friends, their brothers and sisters, parents, teachers and role models.' For more than two decades HIV/AIDS has been tearing families apart.

HIV/AIDS

HIV Stands for *Human Immunodeficiency Virus*, and AIDS stands for *Acquired Immune Deficiency Syndrome*. People affected are exposed to and incubate HIV, producing antibodies which attempt to overcome the intruding virus. However, when the virus is produced at a faster rate than the immune system can cope with, the I IV renders the immune system useless.

Some people carry the virus without ill effect. These people are said to be *exposed-unaffecteds*. In others, a cluster of symptoms (or *syndrome*) is observed, often referred to as *AIDS Related Complex* (or ARC). Where symptoms do appear, they may take from weeks to months to do so and vary in severity. These symptoms include:

- several weeks of excessive tiredness;
- a number of weeks of fever and night sweats;
- repetitious episodes of diarrhoea without an obvious cause;
- cough and shortness of breath which doesn't seem to go away;
- hard pink/purple/dark blotchy skin especially of the mouth and eyes;
- a shingle-like rash on the abdomen, chest and back;
- swollen glands, in the armpits and neck area especially;
- unexpected weight loss (over 4.5kg/10lb over a two-month period).

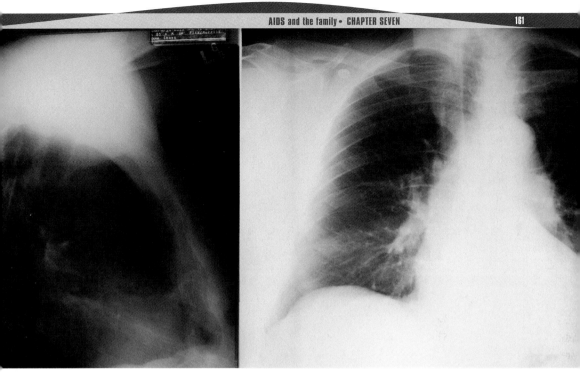

As these symptoms worsen people affected develop serious complications particularly affecting the central nervous system, the digestive system, and the lungs. In many cases HIV/AIDS patients develop *Kaposi's sarcoma* (a rare skin cancer) and/or *pneumocystis carinii* pneumonia.

Early symptoms may occur from 1 to 4 weeks after exposure to HIV. This may be followed by a short or extended period during which the virus is latent (from months to years) before severe symptoms develop. As the immune system becomes increasingly impaired the body becomes less able to defend itself against bacterial, fungal, parasitic, and other viral infections. These infections which, in the absence of HIV may be either naturally resisted or be cleared by medication, develop into the conditions with which they are normally associated and kill the individual. Since these infections, in people with HIV, cannot be met and defended against by the immune system they are referred to as *opportunistic infections*.

People developing opportunistic infections are said to have 'full-blown' AIDS. They may also experience *AIDS dementia complex* (ADC) with:
- loss of concentration;
- confusion and some memory loss;
- weakness in the legs and loss of balance;
- depression, withdrawal, apathy;
- anxiety.

Over time people with ADC have Alzheimer-like conditions, and become incontinent and bedridden.

In societies in which hygiene is minimal due to poverty, opportunistic infections such as tuberculosis take their toll in the community. Rather than acknowledge HIV/AIDS in the family and risk stigmatisation families prefer to say that their loved one died of TB or malaria or whatever.

The viral load of the person with HIV/AIDS will determine the life expectancy as low, medium or high risk. No one has seen the human immunodificiency virus. Persons exposed to HIV risk are tested, where testing facilities are available, for the antibodies present in the blood. There are two main tests for antibodies and some newer tests which are variations of the same chemical procedures: the **ELISA** and **Western Blot** (WB) tests. In the absence of these tests HIV infection is assumed where a combination of ARC is observed, and the person is treated accordingly with drugs to reduce the viral load.

Currently there is no cure for AIDS, and attempts to develop a vaccine have not proved successful. The drugs used are those developed to boost the immune system and slow the viral load of the infected person. Many of these drugs have severe side-effects; need to be taken in large quantities, and at specific times; and must not be missed even for short periods of time. Missing treatment – known as taking a 'drug-holiday' – can provide an opportunity for the virus to mutate into another form for which the prescribed treatment when returned to is useless.

For people who do not have access to treatment the outlook is bleak, hence the very high death-rates for HIV/AIDS worldwide. The cost and availability of drugs will be a life-or-death matter for a considerable portion of the world's population. As the virus mutates at a fairly rapid rate into new forms, many of the existing treatments will not be of benefit in any case.

Although HIV is largely sexually transmitted it can also infect others having contact with the body fluids – blood, semen, and breast milk – of people who are

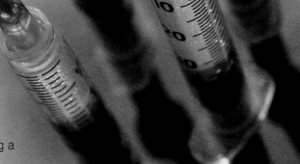

infected. Consequently, drug users sharing needles are at particular risk. In most cases simple hygiene measures are usually sufficient to minimise the risk as HIV has an extremely short life when exposed to the air, antimicrobials, and disinfectants. It is not passed on by kissing or normal body contact.

HIV has more readily infected some people than others. These include young girls and boys in whom the genital tissues are still immature; women who have been genitally mutilated as part of some cultural practices; and homosexual males since anal tissue does not provide natural protection.

Unfortunately, in some marriages women are not in a position to insist on protected sex:
- men working away from home demand unprotected sex when they are at home;
- some gender-biased religions do not give women a voice in their society;
- arranged marriages with no prior knowledge of the intended spouse's premarital sexual activities may place the woman at risk.

While condoms are not one hundred per cent protective, their use may still prevent the trans-mission of HIV.

Condoms should be of thick material for greater protection. Used with a spermicide these arrangements should be adequate.

Social impacts of AIDS

Aside from the considerable physical toll that AIDS takes on the individuals concerned, it also has a dramatic effect on the Community and its ability to function beneficially:
- access to healthcare and education may be reduced;
- the labour pool is reduced, hitting workers hardest in agriculture and among skilled labour, including teachers and health workers;
- poverty increases;
- the infrastructure deteriorates;
- community mortality is elevated;
- loss of resources for mutual aid occurs;
- a general loss of community resilience is felt.

In countries in which families tend to be large and caring and rally round when neighbours face difficulties, HIV/AIDS has completely altered the structure of society. Parents and grandparents lose the support they could

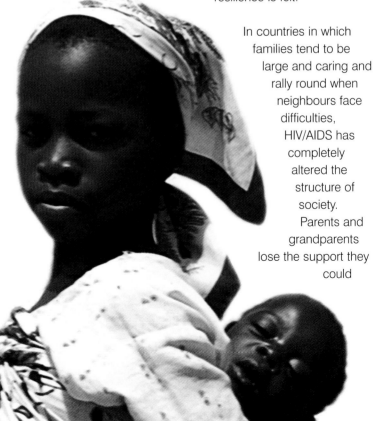

have relied on in their old age. Grandparents are now becoming parents to their grandchildren in the absence of their own children, and many of the older generation can expect to outlive their grandchildren.

With 3.2 million children having AIDS and 15.6 million made orphans, the impact of AIDS on children is overwhelming and includes the following effects:
- loss of   – identity and family
  - health care, immunisation, etc, increased illness vulnerability
  - inheritance, if any due
- psychological distress
- homelessness, with its potential for starvation, vagrancy, and criminality in order to survive
- increased malnutrition
- increased labour demands, long hours and poor pay
- forced immigration
- early exposure to HIV infection through child prostitution

In the belief that having sex with a young virgin will protect against HIV, men in some societies take young brides and themselves transmit HIV to the girls concerned. In other places relatives sell girls into prostitution. Girls and women run the risk of rape, especially in times of war, thus increasing HIV risk. Orphaned children are sometimes separated from their familiar environment by being sold as cheap labour, thus placing these children in risk conditions.

Knowledge for protection
Against the background of the development of HIV/AIDS the UNICEF • UNAIDS • WHO agencies clearly state:

YOUNG PEOPLE HAVE THE RIGHT TO KNOW

- **about sex and their sexuality;**
- **the basic facts on HIV/AIDS and have the necessary life skills to protect themselves from HIV and other STDs;**
- **their HIV status;**
- **how to protect themselves if they are living with HIV/AIDS;**
- **where to get medical, emotional and psychological support if they are living with HIV/AIDS;**
- **how to protect their peers and families from HIV;**
- **how to protect those in their communities who are living with HIV/AIDS;**
- **about (and participate in) HIV education programmes tailored for youth;**
- **their rights and entitlements, and the commitments that governments have made to them;**
- **how to claim and realise these rights.**

Knowing and understanding these basic rights call for a dialogue between those who know and those who need to know and should not have to be hard fought for. Prime Minister Pascoal Mocumbi, of Mozambique, says, 'Above all, we must summon the courage to talk frankly and constructively about sexuality. We must recognise the pressures on our children to have sex that is neither safe nor loving. We must provide them with information, communication skills and, yes, condoms.' It is the last point regarding condoms that has to some extent muted the voice of the faith communities in giving advice to adults and young people. There is a fear that condoning the use of condemns is tacit approval of the promiscuity associated with their use. Until faith communities and parents come to terms with this issue they may unwittingly contribute to the HIV problem in their

communities and families. Young people must be encouraged to delay sexual activity. However, when they do become sexually active, they need to know the ABCs of prevention:

A Abstain from sex/delay the first sexual experience;

B Be faithful to one partner;

C Consistently use a latex condom properly.

The social conditions which become the breeding ground for AIDS are slowly being recognised. Manoj Kurian, writing as a guest editor in the *contact* magazine AIDS issue (Oct-Dec 2000), says that the AIDS pandemic has dramatically exposed a spectrum of gross flaws in our societies:

- an increasingly deep abyss between rich and poor, along with the lack of commitment to bridge it;

- non-availability of basic health services, and the collapse of existing healthcare systems in many countries;
- lack of women's rights; opportunities to resist infection; and an inability to assert reproductive choices or to demand safer sex;
- a long and deafening silence of faith communities, civil society and respective leadership to face up to preventive aspects of HIV/AIDS and other sexuality issues;
- the rise in injecting drug users in many countries and a lowering of the age at which people start injecting.

The Faith Community family

The fifty-two churches and church-related organisations of the Ecumenical Advocacy Alliance (EAA) and Faith Based Organisations (FBO) present at the UN General Assembly Special Session on HIV/AIDS 2002 recognised their unique position in being able to play a role in AIDS prevention:

- they have historical and socio-cultural roots which can be used as effective channels for communication;
- they have the capacity for home-based care for people living with HIV/AIDS and for affected children;
- they have a spiritual mandate in that they can

address the spiritual needs of those affected by HIV/AIDS and so provide a holistic approach to healing;
- they have a demonstrated commitment to respond to human needs.

On the basis of this recognition of their role FBOs are encouraged to:

- eliminate traditional and cultural inequalities especially in the context of women and children;
- ensure that all people living with or affected by HIV/AIDS are receiving the highest possible level of care, respect, love and solidarity;
- raise the consciousness of leaders and members at all levels and train them on HIV/AIDS prevention and care;
- advocate fair and equal access to care and treatments.

Governments must:

- provide extensive support to FBOs (access to information, training and financial resources);

- acknowledge and promote community involvement in prevention efforts, including community-based health care;
- continue all efforts for debt relief of highly indebted countries and ensure that a significant portion of these funds are used in the fight against AIDS;
- ensure access to life-saving/enhancing drugs for the treatment of HIV/AIDS and its opportunistic infections (including antiretroviral drugs).

significant financial and human resources among their own network;
- monitor the UN Global AIDS Fund in order to ensure that it is adequate and efficiently used;
- encourage the use of debt cancellation resources for multi-sectoral HIV/AIDS response.

The EAA encourages churches to:
- facilitate open discussions on HIV/AIDS

The EAA itself will:
- ensure that the levels and channels of funding are responding appropriately to the scale of the HIV/AIDS pandemic;
- urge governments to dedicate increased and sufficient funds;
- ask church and church-related organisations to raise and share

infected and affected people in all church activities;
- value the participation of HIV/AIDS infected and affected people in all church activities;
- become welcoming communities of care for persons infected and affected by HIV/AIDS;

- foster the active participation of women in developing and planning the churches' activities related to HIV/AIDS;
- develop strategies and mobilise constituencies to advocate for more just and effective public policies of governments, international organisations and institutions.

The EAA is especially concerned to:
- break the silence that surrounds issues of sex, sexuality, and sexual relationships;
- support effective (and ethical) methods of prevention;
- eliminate double standards and male dominance, which contribute greatly to women's vulnerability to HIV/AIDS;
- press for the need to understand clearly and address the factors that make children and youth vulnerable to HIV/AIDS.

With the help of all its partners the EAA wishes to:
- strengthen and expand existing health services, infrastructure and human capacity to make the appropriate utilisation of available therapies possible;
- to pressurise governments and pharmaceutical companies to implement policies that allow increased access to live-saving/enhancing drugs (including the antiretrovirals and treatments for opportunistic infections);
- increase availability of services focusing on reproductive health for women and provide access to effective treatment for HIV-infected women;
- prevent 'parent-to-child' transmission.

Adapted from *contact* No. 171, Oct/Dec 2000

Each Faith Based Organisation can, in the light of these aims, play a role in reducing the incidence and the impact of HIV/AIDS. There is still the deep-rooted

matter of stigma to deal with. Being open, honest and understanding is a good start. However, there are other steps that must be taken.

Healthcare workers need to:
- ensure codes of ethics and professional conduct, and other sufficient forms of redress for professional violations;
- encourage practical and attitudinal HIV-related training for all healthcare providers. Promote voluntary counselling and testing (where facilities exist) and care;
- establish and mainstream HIV/AIDS care within the existing health systems and develop discharge and referral systems.

Faith Based Organisations need to:
- provide HIV/AIDS training in basic and ongoing formation for all religious leaders, including counselling skills so that these leaders will be

'AIDS-competent';
- identify and eliminate expressions in religious language and doctrines that are stigmatising, and promote alternative non-judgemental language;
- integrate holistic care and support programmes including life-skills for youth, home-based family care, and support groups for affected persons;
- promote humanitarian and spiritual values of compassion for marginalised and stigmatised groups.

Building on the family foundation
Clearly much of what is expressed in a corporate sense can be part of family life and values. As children grow up in homes where these values are promoted there is a natural acceptance of others regardless of their circumstances. Indeed the fully integrated loving family is the foundation upon which the caring

community is built. As in the family so in society, what hurts one hurts all.

A caring family is a teaching unit for the community. It works both ways. John D. Dupree and Stephen Beck, writing in a WHO publication state, 'One of the most significant factors influencing knowledge, attitudes and behaviour in relation to AIDS is acquaintance with someone who is known to be infected with HIV, or with that person's family, friends, and fellow workers.' They also say, 'If individuals or decision-makers can see and meet people who are affected by the epidemic, particularly people with whom they can identify in some way, they are more likely to see the problems as their own.' A family mentoring a risk-free life in the community will have untold influence for good.

A Church statement helps put the above into context:

Human sexuality is God's gift to humanity. God created sexuality and called it 'very good'. In our sexuality we experience God's love. Giving, serving another, intimately sharing love with another is the biblical view of human sexuality. Biblical sexuality prevents the trivialising of sex and the consequent exposure to HIV infection.

AIDS is preventable by absorbing Christian values and by avoiding sexual contact before marriage and maintaining a faithful, monogamous relationship with an uninfected partner in marriage for life.

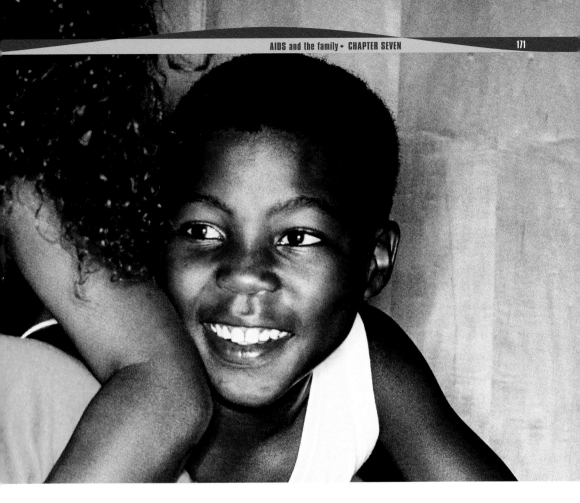

Families need to come to an understanding about such issues as sinning; what it means to be a sinner; stigma and being stigmatised; confession and repentance; sexuality; gender; love, dignity and compassion.

You cannot get AIDS by:

- **shaking hands with an infected person;**
- **eating out in a restaurant;**
- **using public telephones, pools or toilets;**
- **contact with a doctor or dentist who has been treating someone with AIDS;**
- **someone coughing or sneezing near you;**
- **hugging a person;**
- **mosquito or other insect bites;**
- **cuddling pets.**

So there is really no reason for not treating an AIDS-infected person as you would any other person. The isolation of AIDS can be broken with a handshake or a hug, and the person made to feel valued and wanted. Many AIDS-infected persons suffer not only their disease but the social upheaval to their lives. With the death of parents, older children are often proxy parents to their brothers and sisters. Their burdens (including financial) can be eased by caring friends. If there are any values worth learning and sharing it is those acquired in a close, loving family environment. Someone nearby may be waiting for the touch that opens a whole new world to them. We are just a touch away from being part of the healing process.

Richard Willis has worked with sexually-transmitted diseases in Special Treatment Centres while serving in the medical branch of the Royal Navy. He sat his professional qualification in STD at University College Hospital, London, and has subsequently worked and travelled in Africa.

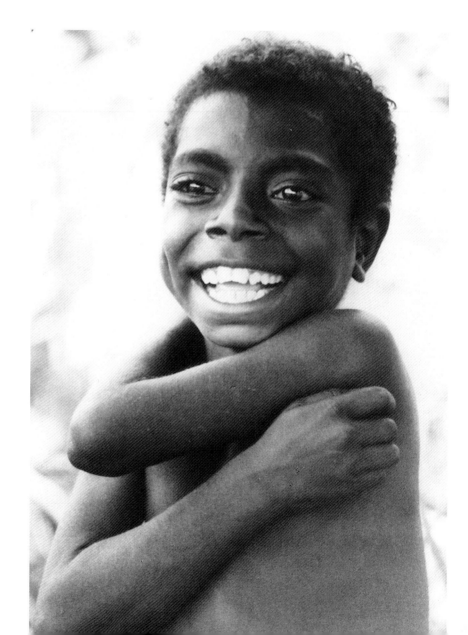

Resources for Chapter 4

Care for the Family
PO Box 488
Cardiff
CF15 7YY

www.care-for-the-family.org.uk
mail@cff.org.uk

CPO (Christian Publicity Organisation)
CPO
Garcia Estate
Canterbury Road
Worthing
W. Sussex
BN13 1BW

www.cpo.org.uk
sales@cpo.org.uk

Intimate Life Ministries
(Keeping Marriages Healthy)
ILM Great Commandment Ministries
PO Box 3065
Warwick
CV34 6DW

mail@greatcommandment.org.uk

The Marriage Course
The Marriage Course
HTB – Brompton Road
London
SW1 1JA

www.themarriagecourse.org
familylife@htb.org.uk

Marriage Partnership Magazine
MasterPlan Publishing
Thames House
63-67 Kingston Road
New Malden Surrey
KT3 3PB

www.mastersun.co.uk
www.marriagepartnership.com